EBAY SELLER SECRETS

2021 EDITION

*Tips & Tricks To Help You Take Your
Reselling Business To The Next Level*

By Ann Eckhart

TABLE OF CONTENTS

INTRODUCTION

I f you read my book BEGINNERS GUIDE TO SELLING ON EBAY, you know that I began my Ebay selling career in 2005 when I needed to liquidate some excess inventory from my home-based gift basket business. I had never sold anything on Ebay before that, so I was shocked at how quickly I was able to sell my overstocked business items!

After selling off my extra gift basket supplies, I cleared out my closets of unwanted clothing and accessories, all of which sold on Ebay quickly and for great prices. I then began searching for more things I could sell online. I soon discovered that many of my gift basket suppliers also sold stand-alone gift products such as ceramics, stuffed animals, and books. So, I slowly started ordering those items to sell on Ebay (the first items being Garfield Christmas ornaments that a company was clearancing out!), and everything that I listed was such a hit that I had quit the gift basket business by the end of the year and focused solely only selling new gift items on Ebay. I eventually expanded to Amazon, and for a few years, my Amazon sales actually outnumbered my Ebay sales ten-to-one.

As the years wore on, however, the online selling landscape changed. Not only were more and more businesses jumping online themselves, everyone from traditional brick-and-mortar retailers to antique deals who had been selling in malls and flea markets, but even the wholesale companies that I had been order-

ing from began selling online directly to customers themselves. Before long, I was pushed out of the gift business entirely and had to find another business strategy. Fortunately, I had a back-up plan.

From time to time, while I was still selling new gifts, I had also purchased things at garage sales and thrift stores to resell on Ebay. When the time came that my new gift products were no longer an option for me to sell, I dove headfirst into "picking" (or "reselling," as most people now call it). My weekends were spent going to every garage sale and estate sale I could find, and my business found a whole new life by focusing on selling vintage treasures, collectibles, home décor, electronics, and pre-owned clothing.

However, regardless of whether I was selling new gifts or second-hand items, I always tried to maintain the same level of stellar customer service and business practices that I had implemented when I first began my business. I learned a lot about what worked and what didn't when selling online with trial and error. In all of my years of selling on Ebay, I have acquired lots of tips and tricks to increase sales and level up my business, all of which I am sharing with you in this book!

Too many Ebay sellers focus only on sourcing products and making money, but a lot goes into running and maintaining a successful Ebay business. Ebay is a unique marketplace. You can run *Auctions* or sell items at *Fixed Price*, and there are *Buy It Now* and *Best Offer* options available. Customers can leave you feedback that can either boost or destroy your business. You can run your entire Ebay business from your smartphone or use multiple devices. And there are numerous shipping carriers to choose from. While all of these choices can seem overwhelming, there are lots of little things you can do to make the Ebay selling process go smoothly, resulting in more sales and more money!

From writing listings and taking photographs to answering customer questions and handling returns, this book is filled with everything I know how to do in order to take your Ebay business to the next level. These are all actions I have taken over the years to keep customers happy and keep growing my sales. All of the advice in this book is straightforward and easy to implement, and I sincerely hope you can use these tips and tricks yourself to increase your reselling income!

CHAPTER ONE:
FROM BEGINNER TO
PROFESSIONAL

B efore we jump into the finer points and details of selling on Ebay, let's first cover some of the basic things you need to do in order to scale up your business. Think of this chapter's advice as the foundation blocks for taking your Ebay business to the next level!

Equipment: The first three pieces of equipment you must have to sell on Ebay are a **computer**, **printer**, and **digital camera or smartphone.** You also need internet access and a strong working knowledge of computers. While you do not need to know programming or Html code to sell online, Ebay is a web-based business that is run via the internet; so, not only do you need to be comfortable with the internet, computers, and printers, you also have to actually own these tools.

Having an efficient computer set up for your Ebay business may seem completely obvious to most people. Still, I can't tell you how many times I have been approached by someone asking me how they can sell on Ebay....without a computer! Or by people who have no idea how even to use one! And even some experienced Ebay sellers still struggle with running their business on outdated equipment.

If you started your Ebay business with a basic computer, printer, and camera, now is the time to consider investing in new models. A computer with a high-speed processor can shave hours off your listing and printing time. A fast-producing printer or a thermal printer can save you time and money. And a quality camera or smartphone will improve your photos. If, like me, you use an iPhone for photographing and creating drafts using the Ebay app, consider an upgrade to the latest model. The benefit of having a smartphone is that you can utilize the Ebay App when you are away from your computer. I use my iPhone to photograph, create drafts, and answer customer questions.

If you are still typing using the one-finger typing method, consider upgrading your word processing skills. These days you can find "How To Type" websites through a simple Google search. Most community colleges and libraries also offer typing classes. The faster you can type out your Ebay listing titles and descriptions, the quicker your items will be listed for sale. After all, things cannot sell if they aren't listed; and nothing is more frustrating than battling a slow computer processor when you are trying to list your items on Ebay.

If you've been using an InkJet printer, it's time to upgrade to at least a LaserPrinter, if not a thermal printer such as a DYMO Label or Zebra Label printer. These printers are not only specifically designed to print shipping labels, but because they are thermal printers, they don't use ink, which is a huge savings. I, myself, am content with my HP LaserPrinter and using label sheets for my postage; but if you are consistently shipping ten or more items a day, a thermal printer will likely save you time and money in the long run.

Remember that any money you spend on your Ebay business equipment can be deducted as an expense come tax time. Be sure to track everything you purchase and keep the receipts so that you can claim maximum deductions. I will be discussing how to manage your Ebay accounting later on in this book.

Internet: Reliable internet access is critical to selling on Ebay. I pay $50 a month for high-speed internet access. If you have been getting by with basic service with a slow connection, now is the time to look into upgrading to high-speed broadband internet service. Call your current internet provider and ask how the available options to upgrade your service. Just as a faster computer and better printer will save you time, so will high-speed internet. And just as those equipment expenses can be written off at tax time, so can your internet bill.

Space: As you already know, Ebay inventory, shipping supplies, and a workstation can take up a lot of room, even if you are only selling on a part-time basis. To take your Ebay business to the next level, you likely need to expand your space or at least better organize it. I have an office in the upstairs of my home where I photograph, create listings, and process orders. However, my actual inventory, as well as my massive supply of shipping boxes and envelopes, are in my basement. And the rest of my shipping supplies (tape, packing paper, bubble wrap, etc.) are in the corner of my living room.

If you want to take your Ebay business to the next level, now is the time to consider devoting an entire room (or rooms!) to your business. If you have a spare bedroom or a basement, you will want to look into using them as dedicated inventory and shipping spaces. Also, consider garages, closets, and unused corners of rooms to utilize for your business.

If you are completely out of room in your home, you may want to consider renting a storage locker or even an office. However, you should exhaust all of the available space within your own home before taking on the added expense of an off-site office.

Postage Scale: If you do not already have a digital postage scale for your Ebay business, put this book down and buy one, either from a local office supply store or online from Amazon or Ebay.

These scales cost less than $20, which is a small price for an item that will save you time and money in the long run as you'll be able to print out the postage for orders from your home. If you aren't willing to purchase a digital scale for your Ebay shipping, then you should stop reading this book and resign yourself to hauling all of your packages to the Post Office.

Shipping Supplies: Shipping requires shipping supplies, and that means shipping boxes and envelopes. When selling on Ebay, you need two forms of shipping boxes/envelopes:

- **Priority Mail boxes and envelopes for Priority Mail**
- **Plain boxes and envelopes for Media Mail, First Class Mail, and Parcel Select.**

You've likely already got a stash of boxes and envelopes on hand, but now it's time to increase your supply. Fortunately, the United States Postal Service (USPS) offers **FREE Priority Mail shipping boxes**. Not only can you order regular *Priority* boxes and envelopes, but you can also order *Flat Rate* boxes and envelopes. I keep the following *Priority Mail* products, all of which are FREE and were delivered for FREE to my home, on hand at all times:

<u>Standard Priority:</u>

- **Priority Mail Show Box OSHOEBOX** - 14-7/8 x 7-3/8 x 5.24 (not just for shoes, but for anything long and narrow)
- **Priority Mail Box 1097** - 11-5/8 x 2.5x 13-7/16 (rectangle size for clothing, books, and anything flat)
- **Priority Mail Box 1905** – 12.5 x 3-1/8 x 15-5/8 (rectangle size for clothing, books, and anything flat)
- **Priority Mail Box 1092** – 12.25 x 2-7/8 x 13-11/16 (rectangle size for clothing, books, and anything flat)
- **Priority Mail Box 1096L** – 9-7/16 x 6-7/16 x 2-3/16 (rectangle size for clothing, books, and anything flat)
- **Large Priority Mail Box 7** – 12.25 x 12.25 x 1.5 (largest size of the Priority Mail boxes; perfect for shipping sev-

eral items at once)
- **Priority Mail Box 4** – 7.25 x x7.25 x 6.25 (square size is perfect for shipping mugs, figurines, and small, rounded items)

Flat-Rate Priority:

- **Priority Mail Padded Flat Rate Envelope** – 9.5 x 12.5 (the go-to choice for shipping heavy clothing, shoes, and anything unbreakable)
- **Priority Mail Small Flat Rate Box** – 8-11/16 x 5-7/16 x 1.75 (sized for small but heavy items)
- **Priority Mail Medium Flat Rate Box 1** – 11.25 x 8.75 x 6 (perfect size for mid-size, heavy objects)
- **Priority Mail Medium Flat Rate Box 2** – 12 x 3.5 x 14-1/8 (the flat, rectangle version of the size above)
- **Priority Mail Large Flat Rate Box LARGEFRB** – 12.25 x 12.25 x 6 (this box is smaller than the regular Large Priority Mail Box, but it can still come in handy for smaller, heavier items)
- **Priority Mail Regional Rate Box A1** – 10-1/8 x 7-1/8 x 5 (postage for the Regional Rate boxes are often cheaper than their regular Flat Rate counterparts)
- **Priority Rate Regional Rate Box A2** – 11-1/16 x 2.5 x 13-1/16 (the rectangle version of the Regional Rate A1 box)

Stickers: (*these are perfect for covering writing on the outside of re-purposed boxes*)

- **Priority Mail Sticker Label 107 Roll of 250**
- **Priority Mail Sticker Label 107R Roll of 1000**
- **Priority Mail Shipping Label 106 Pack of 10**

When you are looking through all of the available choices for *Priority Mail* boxes and envelopes, you will see that USPS offers many other options that I didn't list above. As you continue along your Ebay journey, you will learn which shipping boxes and envelopes that you use the most, and therefore, need to reorder frequently. While the above selections are the products that I use the most often, here are some other ones you may want to consider adding to your supply:

- **Priority Mail Express Boxes & Envelopes**: I do not offer Express or Overnight options to my customers (and I have only ever had one person ask me to ship something faster than Priority), so for me, I don't bother keeping any of these products stocked. If I needed to send something via Express, I would likely just take it to the Post Office packaged in a plain box and have them put the label and Express stickers on it.
- **Tube Boxes:** If you sell posters and/or prints, these tube boxes are great.
- **Envelopes:** There are several options for flat envelopes, but whenever I want to send something that would fit in one of these options, I ship it in a Padded Flat Rate. These envelopes are geared towards businesses that frequently mail documents, such as law, banking, and medical offices.
- **Regional Rate B Boxes:** For me, Regional Rate A boxes are always the cheapest option. The B boxes' benefit is that they can ship up to 20 pounds, while the A boxes are maximum of 15 pounds for domestic shipments. However, I've never had to ship anything that heavy that would fit in any of the Regional Rate boxes, regardless.

The Post Office offers its free shipping supplies in quantities as low as ten each. I recommend that you order the smallest number possible as you expand your collection. You will soon realize which boxes you use the most, but you will at least have the others on hand if you need them. Note that sometimes it can take quite a while for boxes to be delivered due to supply issues; so, don't wait until you are completely out to order more, especially heading into the busy holiday season. I make sure I order my supply of *Priority Mail* boxes in September in anticipation of the fourth quarter.

While *Priority Mail* is an excellent option for shipping most packages, you will need other forms of packaging for **Media Mail, First Class Mail,** and **Parcel Select,** as those selections can NOT be mailed in the *Priority Mail* boxes. It is also against USPS policy to alter the *Priority* boxes in any way, so forget thinking you can turn them inside out (they are printed with *Priority Mail* on the inside to thwart this) or put stickers on the outside to conceal the fact that they are indeed *Priority*. Misusing USPS supplies can result in your losing your postal account.

Before you run out and buy new shipping boxes and envelopes, check around your house to see what you have on hand. Plain cardboard boxes, manila envelopes, and bubble mailers can all be used for non-priority mail. If you already have items on hand that you intend to list on Ebay, look them over to determine the packaging you need. Perhaps you are only going to sell books, for which bubble mailers and sturdy boxes are enough. On the other hand, if you only plan to sell large items, you don't need to worry about stocking up on envelopes.

I keep a wide variety of boxes and envelopes in my shipping supply area. While I utilize the free *Priority Mail* boxes and bubble mailers from the Post Office, I invest in plain shipping boxes from Amazon, Ebay, Uline, and Value Mailers for *Media, First Class,* and *Parcel* packages; and I purchase branded shipping supplies directly from Ebay. I also have manila bubble mailer envelopes that I buy at Sam's Club and poly mailers that I order on Amazon. I keep the following plain boxes and envelopes on hand:

- **Plain Cardboard Shipping Boxes** (4", 6", 8", 10", and 12" sizes)
- **Oversized Cardboard Shipping Boxes** (14" and 16" sizes for when I have to ship oversized items via Parcel or UPS)
- **Poly Mailers in various sizes** (for shipping clothing)

- **Bubble Mailers in various sizes** (for items that need more cushioning than a plain poly mailer)
- **Cardboard Mailers in various sizes** (for shipping coloring books, stickers, and other items that I don't want bent in the mail)

Note that because I have been selling on Ebay for years and am set up as a business, I can buy these supplies and then deduct them as business expenses. As you begin to purchase more shipping supplies and office equipment, be sure to track your spending as you can deduct these costs come tax time. This is why I try to limit the places I buy supplies from as I can simply scan my credit card statements to find my monthly expenses.

Packing Materials: You cannot just throw an item into a box and ship it with no packing materials to buffer it inside of the box (well, you CAN, as I have seen many sellers do, but you shouldn't). You need to WRAP up your items to protect them inside of the box. You want to ensure that the item is protected from being thrown around, both inside of planes and trucks, as well as being tossed onto customer's porches. I invest in the following packing materials for my Ebay orders:

- **Recycled Packing Paper** (to wrap up items inside of the shipping box)
- **Bubble Wrap** (essential for protecting breakables such as China and ceramics)
- **Packing Peanuts** (perfect for buffering breakables inside of boxes)
- **Shipping Tape** (buy the largest rolls and the strongest type you can)
- **Tissue Paper** (better than packing paper for wrapping delicate breakables)
- **Cardboard Corrugated Rolls** (allows you to create a box-in-a-box around breakables)

Let's say we are shipping out a coffee mug. The first thing we would do would be to wrap the mug in a layer of bubble wrap.

We would then wrap a strip of cardboard around the outside before wrapping another bubble wrap layer around that. Finally, we would cushion the mug further by using packing peanuts all around it inside the shipping box, making sure that there is a good distance between the shipping box wall and the item itself. This is considered the box-in-a-box method as we have essentially created a box around the item before placing it in yet another box.

Shipping Station: By now, in your Ebay journey, you have likely accumulated a lot of shipping materials. And if you haven't done so already, it is time to get serious about organizing everything into one centrally located shipping station area. An out of the way corner of a room or basement is ideal for this. Remember that just as you want to protect your inventory from household and pet smells, you also want to ensure that your shipping supplies are kept away from smoke, pet dander, and other odors.

The ideal shipping station will contain all of your supplies within arms reach. A large table is necessary for providing you enough space to package up orders on a flat service. Industrial shelving units are perfect for holding heavy shipping boxes. Packing peanuts are best stored in a plastic tote, while bubble wrap and cardboard wrap can stay on their rolls until you need to cut off the desired amount. Your packing paper and tissue paper should be readily available, and organizing your scissors, tape, and other small supplies on a tableside cart or portable bin ensures they are handy.

Be sure you have the tools, skills, and space you need to obtain, list, store, and ship your items. You want your focus to be on making money, not wasting time waiting for your slow computer to print labels or searching for a shipping box.

Managed Payments: As of this writing, most Ebay sellers are now enrolled in Ebay's *Managed Payments. Managed Payments* is Ebay's payment processing system; it works just like PayPal did. PayPal was Ebay's payment processing system since the website launched, but the two companies split in 2018. *Managed Pay-*

ments allows customers to purchase items directly on the Ebay site without being directed to use their PayPal accounts. In short, buyers can now shop on Ebay the same way they do on most other websites. And just like PayPal, buyers can pay via *Managed Payments* using various methods, including credit cards, debit cards, bank accounts, and even PayPal.

But for Ebay sellers, *Managed Payments* means that Ebay, not PayPal, now manage their funds. When someone purchases one of your items on Ebay, Ebay will process their payment, deduct the fees and shipping costs (after you have printed off the shipping label) associated with the transaction, and then disperse the remaining funds to you. You can choose to have your funds dispersed daily or weekly.

To check on your **Managed Payments** statistics, simply go to your **Seller Hub** and click on the **Payments** tab at the top of the page.

Here you will find detailed breakdowns of **Your Financial Summary**, including:

Total Funds: Here, you can see your available funds as well as pending funds. You will also see your next payout amount as well as your last payout amount. You can choose to have your money dispersed daily or weekly.

Invoice: When a buyer pays for an item, Ebay immediately deducts the selling fees. The shipping cost is also deducted after the postage is purchased. However, as of this writing, your monthly *Store Subscription Fee* is NOT deducted from your balance. So, under *Invoice,* you will see the current amount due along with any other fees not yet invoiced. You will see your *Last payment received* and your *Next invoice* date.

You can also *Make a one-time payment* from a third-party funding source such as your bank account, credit card, debit card, or PayPal account. This is a frustrating change for me as I used to pay all of my fees, including my store subscription, from my PayPal account. But now, my store subscription fees are charged to my credit card every month. Hopefully, Ebay will eventually enable our store fees to be deducted from our balances the way both Amazon and Etsy do for their sellers.

Recent Transactions: At the bottom of the page, Ebay will show you your *Recent transactions*, including the date, order number, title, and price for each item you sold as well as the fees and shipping label charges that were taken out of your pending balance.

Settings: Under *Settings* are your current **Payout method, Payout schedule, Automatic payment method,** and **Backup payout method.** This section gives you easy access if you want to alter any of the funding/payout sources you have on file.

All Transactions: On the left-hand side of the *Payments* section of *Seller Hub* is a column of links, beginning with **All Transactions.** Clicking this link will take you to a list of the items you have sold and their associated fees. You can narrow down this information by *status, type, order number,* or a *keyword/phrase* you manually enter in. You can also change the time-frame from *Last 30 days, Last 60 days, Last 90 days,* or *Custom.*

Payouts: Going back to the left-hand column, you can click on *Payouts* to see your most recent *Managed Payment* disbursements from Ebay into your bank account.

Expenses: Clicking on the *Expenses* link will take you to a list of the fees and postage costs that Ebay has recently deducted from your balance. You can break this list down further by *fee type, time range, order number,* or a *search term* of your choosing.

Reports: Back over on the left-hand column of the page, you will see *Reports*, which is where you can find a wealth of statistics regarding your business. And as a bonus, you can download these reports onto your computer to email your accountant or to print them out for your own records. You can view your *Transaction Reports* or *Payout Reports*, your monthly *Statements*, and your monthly *Invoices*.

Taxes: Back over on the left-hand column, you will find the link for *Taxes*, which is where you can print out your 1099 tax forms. Note that if you sell $20,000 or more in a year on Ebay, Ebay will issue you a tax form. Most of us will be getting 1099 forms from both PayPal and Ebay for 2020 due to most sellers still being enrolled in PayPal and then *Managed Payments* during the course of the year. However, remember that even if Ebay or PayPal doesn't issue you a tax form, you STILL need to report your IRS earnings. I will be discussing how to handle accounting for your business in the final chapter of this book.

Payout Settings: The second-to-last option on the left-hand column is your *Payout settings*. Here you will be able to view your current settings as well as change them whenever you want. You can edit your *Payout method, Payout schedule, Automatic payment method,* and your *Backup payment method.*

Taxpayer Details: The last link under the *Payments* tab is for your taxpayer settings. This section is still in BETA testing; as of this writing, it takes you to the *My Ebay* section of your account where you can review your business information and account preferences.

All of this data can seem overwhelming, but you must familiarize yourself with your Seller Hub area, especially regarding the money you are earning on Ebay!

CHAPTER TWO:
EXPERT LISTING
TIPS & TRICKS

P icture this: You have just come home from a day of thrifting and have bags full of great stuff you can't wait to get listed on Ebay. The best thing to do is jump right in, take a few pictures, and put everything online as fast as you can, right? WRONG! A lot goes into creating a great Ebay listing that will not only result in you getting the best price but also in a happy customer who leaves you positive feedback.

Up until now, you may have just been listing your items as-is, guessing at prices, and letting the chips fall where they may. But if you really want to scale up your Ebay business, you will want to follow the suggestions below to take your listings to the next level!

Research: Before I list anything on Ebay, I first research it to see what the going price for the item currently is; or if it even selling at all. The way I do this is by doing a completed listing search. I simply type in a general description of my item in the search bar (for instance, "Pink Pyrex Bowl"), and I then narrow down the search fields, which appear on the screen's left side. Included in those search fields is one for **Completed Listings.** Selecting

Completed Listings will show me what, if anything, an item has recently sold for.

If a completed listing search brings up several hundred listings, I will further narrow it down by selecting the **Sold** listings. Instead of showing me every item listed in the past few months, regardless of whether it sold or not, selecting *Sold* will only show me the listings that resulted in a sale. I can then sort the results using several options, including most recently ended, distance, or price; I prefer to sort using the highest price so that I can see which items sold for the most money. Note the price will also include shipping, regardless of whether the buyer or seller paid for it.

Since you are reading this book to grow your Ebay business, I assume that you have or plan to get an Ebay store subscription. I will discuss the benefits of opening an Ebay store later on in this book, but I want to cover now one of the main bonuses of having a store: **Terapeak.**

Ebay acquired *Terapeak*, which is an online database of Ebay sales data in 2017. *Terapeak* is now available for FREE to *Basic, Premium, Anchor,* and *Enterprise* Ebay store subscribers; *Starter* store and non-store sellers can subscribe to the service for $12 per month for the annual plan, or $19 per month with no commitment.

Terapeak takes researching sold Ebay listings up a notch by providing you with an entire year's worth of data. While the *Completed Listing* search on Ebay only gives you three months of sales records, with *Terapeak,* you can see what an item has been selling for during the previous twelve months. This is incredibly useful when you are researching off-season items. For instance, when you are listing Christmas items in May, *Terapeak* will show you what those items were selling for leading up to the previous holiday. I always advocate listing items whenever you have the time, not waiting until a specific season comes around. And if you are willing to sit on an item for a while, *Terapeak* allows you to set the highest selling price and wait for the right buyer to come along.

You can easily access *Terapeak* under the **Research** tab at the top of your **Seller Hub**. Trust me when I tell you that once you start utilizing *Terapeak* to research completed listings, you will never go back to the traditional Ebay search method!

When you are researching sold listings, whether via Terapeak or through Ebay's completed listings search, you will often find that your item has sold for a wide range of prices. This is when you need to examine the results to see why some sold for a high price while others only sold for a few dollars, if at all. Sometimes the reason is because the seller had a low asking price, either starting an item at auction for only 99-cents or listing it at *Fixed Price* for just a few dollars. Perhaps the pictures in the listing were terrible, or maybe the item itself was in awful condition. Compare the highest sold price listing with the lowest one to determine what factored into the difference. And then price your item accordingly.

If my item is in the same condition as the listing that sold for the highest price, I base my price on that listing. I also note *when* the item was sold to account for seasonality. Back to the example of Christmas items: If I am listing a Christmas collectible, I want to base my price on what it sold for during the previous holiday season, not what it may have sold for during the summer months. For some items, specifically vintage collectibles, I'm willing to let them sit in my store until the right buyer comes along. The exception to this is clothing, as I prefer to move clothes much faster, specifically if it is a trendy piece that may go out of style if it is listed too long.

Note that it is imperative to base the selling price of the item you are listing on the comparable sales results and conditions. While a brand-new book may bring in top dollar, a used one may only bring in a few bucks. Ensure that you base your item's price on those in a similar condition to yours when you are looking at the completed listing results. Remember that "brand new" refers to items with absolutely no flaws and with the original tags attached, basically, in the condition it was in as it rolled off the manufacturing line. However, most of the items you will sell on Ebay are likely to be secondhand, and condition plays a huge factor in how much pre-owned items will sell for.

I also use the *Terapeak* and Ebay search results to tell me if an item usually only sells with "free" shipping. As I say in every Ebay book that I have ever written, shipping is never actually "free" as someone, either the seller or the buyer has to pay for the postage. However, some categories, such as clothing, are so crowded and competitive that building the cost of postage into the asking price to list the item with "free" shipping is often necessary to get the sale. Health and beauty items are also products that typically sell best when listed with "free" shipping. And if you sell similar items, offering "free" shipping may help convince a buyer to purchase multiple items from you as they will not be wondering about the shipping charges.

While I typically research pricing on my computer, I sometimes look up items on my smartphone using Ebay's mobile app when I am out and about. That way, I can quickly find if an item is worth me picking up or if I should pass on it. The downside to using Ebay Mobile for me is that I often run into problems finding an internet connection (especially when I am at an estate sale in the country). I have even had difficulty getting an internet connection inside of Goodwill stores. So, while it would be nice to look up every item before I buy it, I often have to rely on instinct and wait until I return to my office to do any research. If the item you are researching has a bar code, you can use the Ebay app to scan it in to check on its current price. Note that if the Ebay app isn't working for you for whatever reason, you can also use the Amazon Seller app for scanning purposes.

Remember that an item is only worth what someone will pay for it. Therefore, looking at the *active* Ebay listings isn't going to be much help as those results only show what sellers are currently ASKING for the item. The *completed listings* will show you what customers have *actually* PAID for the item. This is often the biggest mistake new Ebay sellers make; they are only looking at the active listings, not the sold results. I also hear this a lot from people selling their items at garage sales. "It's selling for $1000 on Ebay!" they will claim, but they've usually only looked at the active listings, not the sold results.

Some categories, specifically clothing, require you to list the size of the item you are selling. While most clothing sizes are straightforward, I sometimes need to research how various clothing brands size their garments. For instance, Chicos, a women's clothing company, has its own unique sizing chart ranging from 000 (extra small) to 4.5 (extra-large). I also often have to research whether a piece of clothing is vintage (say, a pair of Levi's jeans) and how to spot counterfeit items (such as how to tell a real Coach purse from a fake).

I also pick up vintage items from overseas that aren't labeled in English; fortunately, Google can quickly translate most languages to English. I have found several German Bibles and hymnals over the years that I needed help translating, and I've also gotten pottery that was marked in a foreign language. I simply type in the book title or makers mark into the Google search bar, followed by "translate to English" to get a translation.

If you are dealing with vintage and collectible items like me, you may need to do further research on a piece to provide as much information about it as possible. For instance, I sell a lot of vintage flatware sets. These sell best when I can identify the pattern; so, I visit sites such as *replacements.com* to find the name, manufacturer, and date of the sets I am selling.

Again, a simple Google search will bring up all kinds of resources for most objects you are selling. Nearly every collectible item has at least one dedicated website, often run by actual collectors that you can use to research everything from pottery to clothing. Don't just rely on Ebay to do your research; use the World Wide Web to learn as much as you can about the items you are selling.

Yes, all of this research takes time; but remember that the more information you can provide in your listings, the more likely your item will sell fast and for top dollar!

Clean & Repair: When I come home from the thrift store or an estate sale, the first thing I do is lay everything I bought out on a table so that both my dad ("Papa" is my volunteer employee; his unofficial title is "Shipping & Receiving Manager") and I can look everything all over for damage. Even though I always try to inspect items before I buy them, it is not at all uncommon to end up finding ceramics with cracks or clothes with stains once I get them home. This is especially true when I am at a crowded estate sale or if I happen upon a fill-a-bag event.

If we find an item with damage, I have to decide whether it can be repaired or even want to spend the time and energy to fix it. While it is easy to tighten up a loose button, you can't repair a coffee mug with a giant chip in it. If I decide that an item can't be fixed, I either throw it away or donate it to Goodwill. The Goodwill stores in my area advertise that they will take all damaged goods as they recycle broken materials. They also sell bulk pallets of salvage fabric overseas. Before you donate damaged goods to your local thrift store, be sure to check their policy as some just send unsellable items to the dump. If that is the case, see if you can recycle or reuse them on your own. For instance, we cut up damaged clothing and use the scraps as cleaning cloths. I have also put slightly damaged items out on the curb with a "FREE" sign to see if someone can salvage them.

After we have weeded out the damaged goods, we start cleaning the remaining items. The first thing my dad does is to remove all price stickers and tags. He uses "Scotty Peelers," which are labels and sticker removers available with both plastic and metal blades. You can find these on Amazon and Ebay for under $10. For stubborn stickers, my dad will use Goo Gone, nail polish remover, or paint thinner. However, it is essential to be careful when using a chemical to remove stickers as you do not want to damage the

actual item. Some chemicals will also remove the paint or glaze from the surface of the item you are trying to clean. Or, if it is a paper item, trying to remove a label could tear it. In those cases, it is best to either leave the sticker on as-is or use a marker to blot out the price. If it is a vintage item with its original price sticker, I actually prefer to leave it on as it adds charm to the piece.

For items where the price was written in permanent marker directly on the surface (the Goodwill stores in my area are notorious for doing this), we use paint thinner or nail polish remover to wipe it off using a Q-Tip or piece of cloth. Hand sanitizer gel can be used to get marker off of clothing tags. Sometimes marker print comes off easily, whereas other times, you really have to scrub to get it to disappear. Paint thinner, nail polish remover, and old rags are all essential parts of my reselling toolkit!

Once all price stickers have been removed, we wash all ceramics (most are dishwasher safe, which makes the task much easier), carefully dust electronics, thoroughly search and clean out purses and bags, wipe off old books, and wash all clothing (unless it's leather or suede or has the original price tags still attached). While many sellers do not wash clothing before listing it, I prefer to, as I am not sure where the item has been before purchasing it at the thrift store. That way, I am touching clean items when I go to list them; after all, I don't want thrift store residue on me or my desk area.

If a clothing item still has its original tags but has an odor, I will try airing it outside or even put it in the freezer to kill the scent. Some resellers also use steamers to not only smooth out wrinkles but to sanitize their clothing pieces. There is a "thrift store smell" that is often present on thrifted items, and some secondhand shops, including the Goodwill Outlets, spray their items with a solution to kill bed bugs. The chemicals in that spray cause me to have an allergic reaction. So, washing clothing, steaming them, or at the very least airing them out is essential for me.

Taking the time to clean your items will not only help them look

better in photos, but customers who open their package to find clean items will be more likely to leave positive feedback. I take the "Golden Rule" approach to cleaning and repairing the items I sell on Ebay, making them look how I would want them to if I were the customer!

Auction vs. Fixed Price: What makes Ebay such a unique selling platform are all of the different ways you can sell items. You can run **Auctions** from one to ten days, and you can also, for an added fee, include a **Buy It Now** price to your auction listing. Or you can list items at **Fixed Price.** While Ebay used to allow you to list items for a set period, now all *Fixed Price* items are listed **Good 'Till Cancelled.**

Then there is the **Best Offer** option, which you can add to both *Auction* and *Fixed Price* listings. *Best Offer* allows potential buyers to send you a direct offer on your item. You can either accept, decline, or negotiate with a Counteroffer. You can also set up **Automatic Accept** and **Automatic Decline** options to instantly agree to or decline offers that meet or don't meet the thresholds you've set.

There are so many choices, I know! But the bottom line is that all Ebay listings, despite the length and added options, will either be *Auctions* or *Fixed Price.* Many Ebay sellers start out selling their items using one format and get stuck using the same option for all of their listings. However, some items sell better at *Auction* while others do best at *Fixed Price.* But how do you know whether or not you should start an item at *Auction* or just list it at *Fixed Price*? The answer depends on the item itself.

If you have done your research, using either Ebay's *Completed Listing* search or *Terapeak*, and found that the item you are selling commands a steady price of, say, $50 on Ebay, then go ahead and list yours for $50 at *Fixed Price.* If you find your item is selling for a wide range of prices, you may want to price yours in the middle. So, if your item is selling from anywhere between $20 and $60, you may try pricing yours at *Fixed Price* for $40 to ensure a quick

sale. As I discussed earlier in this book, condition is a huge factor in pricing your items. If the items you see selling for top-dollar are in like-new condition, but the item you are listing is in poor condition, you need to price accordingly.

However, if you see that the item typically brings in many bidders at *Auction*, you may want to try listing yours at *Auction*, too. While you can run an Ebay *Auction* from one to ten days, I prefer listing them for seven days. Seven days gives potential customers an entire week to find your item listing and to then decide if they want to bid.

As far as adding the *Buy It Now* option to auctions, I rarely do this as you have to pay an additional fee; and I try to keep my Ebay fees as low as possible. If I have a good idea of how much an item will sell for, I just list it at *Fixed Price* rather than bother with an *Auction* as, again, I am only doing *Auctions* for items I have no idea how to price or because I want to get them out of my inventory. Note that if you have a particularly "hot" item that you've started at *Auction*, you will likely receive messages asking you to sell the item outright. This is a tell-tale sign that you should keep the item at *Auction* just as you listed it as it indicates just how desirable it is. And it's also a good reminder that you were smart not to have added a *Buy It Now* option in as the bidding will likely go higher than the price you would have set.

If I think an item should realistically sell for $19.99, I will not list it at *Auction* for $9.99 with a $19.99 *Buy It Now* price as the item would likely end up only selling for $9.99, anyway. And if an item has the potential of selling for $50, I will not start it at an *Auction* of $9.99 with a *Buy It Now* of $19.99 as I am severely limiting my profit potential. In both of these cases, adding in the *Buy It Now* option would not only result in my items likely selling for less money, but I would also have to pay additional listing fees for the extra feature.

While Ebay started off as an auction site, the landscape has changed a lot over the years. It is now really tough to get the price you want for an item when you start it as an *Auction* as customers are becoming used to and now typically prefer to buy things at a set price rather than bidding on something and then having to wait up to a week to see whether or not they win. More than ever before, Ebay is in direct competition with Amazon and Walmart, so you need to continually adjust your selling strategies to meet the changing times.

While I typically stick to listing my Ebay items at *Fixed Price*, I will occasionally use *Auctions* to clear out stale inventory, especially clothing. *Auctions* are an excellent way to bring in traffic to my Ebay store, and even if someone doesn't bid on anything I have up at *Auction*, they may end up checking out my other listings and buying one of my *Fixed Price* items.

Best Offer: When you list an item at *Fixed Price* on Ebay, you have the option of allowing buyers to send you offers via the *Best Offer* feature. There is no additional fee associated with adding the *Best Offer* option to your listings. You can add *Best Offer* to all or only some of your listings, and you can also remove it at any time if you change your mind. It is easy to add *Best Offer* to your listings; you can do so individually within the listing itself by checking the box under the price to enable customers to submit offers to you.

If you want to add *Best Offer* to multiple listings, the **Bulk Edit** feature makes adding and removing options such as *Best Offer* easy; just go to your **Seller Hub** and click on **Listings**. Select **Active** from the drop-down menu and click on the boxes next to the listings you want to edit. Then click on **Edit** and select **Edit Selected** from the drop-down menu. You will then be taken to a page when you can bulk add, edit, or remove features, including price, payment, and shipping.

When dealing with *Best Offer,* note that you can choose to accept or decline offers automatically, or you can choose to review each offer personally. For instance, if you have an item priced at $50, you can choose to accept any offer of $40 or more automatically;

and you can choose to decline any offers under $24.99 automatically. However, as I said, you can leave the settings open to review every offer. Some sellers prefer to review all offers manually and never set up an auto-decline price as they believe that it is best to attempt to negotiate with anyone who sends an offer. However, what you decide to do is up to you.

When you do get an offer on an item, you have 48 hours to review it and respond. You can accept the offer, and the buyer will automatically be committed to completing the purchase. Many Ebay sellers such as myself hope that once all users are enrolled in Ebay's *Managed Payments* system that buyers who submit a *Best Offer* will have their funds automatically sent to the seller rather than having to initiate payment. Poshmark allows buyers to submit offers to sellers. If the seller accepts the offer, Poshmark immediately charges the customer for the purchase and sends the seller a label to ship out the item. On Ebay, however, buyers still have to submit payment manually. And while most customers do pay, there are, of course, those who do not. Hopefully, this is something that Ebay will eventually be able to enact via *Managed Payments.*

Back to receiving a *Best Offer:* Note that you can also outright refuse any offers, which closes the communication between you and the buyer. If that buyer wants to send you another offer, they will have to start the *Best Offer* process again. Some buyers like to send ridiculously low offers, such as offering $1 for a $50 item. These people obviously have no real interest in buying the item, so I do not engage with them; I simply decline their offer. If they are pesky and message me or submit another low offer, I will block them.

However, if you get a reasonable offer, you can choose to send the customer a counteroffer; most sellers do send counteroffers for reasonable offers from buyers who they suspect really want the item. Let's go back to that $50 item. You have it listed at *Fixed Price* with the *Best Offer* option. A potential customer sends you an offer of $30. You can then send a counteroffer of, say, $40. If the buyer accepts, they are then required by Ebay to complete the transaction for the item. However, the customer may want to continue to negotiate by submitting a counteroffer to you of $35; again, you can accept this or counteroffer again yourself, either for your original $40 offer or for one a couple of dollars less, say $38.

Sometimes, however, counteroffers are not accepted or completely ignored. While this can be frustrating, it is just a part of the unique Ebay selling platform. Don't get discouraged by customers who send low-ball offers or refuse your counteroffers; move on, and eventually, the right buyer will come along. Just the fact that someone has engaged with your listing by sending an offer helps the item show up higher in Ebay's search algorithm as the action is telling the Ebay system that people are interested in the item and that it has the potential to sell. And at the end of the day, Ebay is a business; they want your items to sell just as much as you do so that they can charge you *Final Value Fees* on top of your *Insertion Fees* and *Store Subscription Fees.*

Note that you want to carefully review all offers to ensure the offer does not include a change to the shipping price. I have had buyers send me an offer that also stipulated I would give them free shipping. For instance, they would offer me $5 plus free shipping for an item I had listed for $10 with the buyer paying shipping. Had I accepted those terms, I would have essentially had to PAY to ship them the item. So, be very careful to understand the terms you agree to when you accept a *Best Offer.*

As far as adding the *Best Offer* option to my own listings, I only do this after an item has been listed for a month or so. If I list something for $50 and after 30 days it hasn't sold, I might end the listing and then relist it (using the **Sell Similar** option so that the item shows up as a brand-new listing on Ebay's site) but add in the *Best Offer* option. I typically do not do this the first time around as I want to try for the maximum selling price, and when you have the *Best Offer* option active, most customers are likely to try and negotiate.

I personally set my *Best Offer* listings to automatically decline any offer that is less than 50% of my asking price. If I were willing to take half for an item, I would just list it for that. As for which offers I will accept, I look carefully at the item itself, what I originally paid for it, how long I've had it listed, and what I really think it should go for. I will generally accept offers of 25% or less of my asking price; if the offer is between 26-51% of my asking price, I will usually send a counteroffer to try to get closer to the 25% mark. However, some sellers happily engage with any customer who sends offers. What you decide to do is up to you and how much time (and patience!) you have for fielding offers.

I only negotiate sale prices using the official Ebay *Best Offer* feature; I do NOT accept offers or make deals using the Ebay messaging system or with people who email me directly. It is very common for buyers to message sellers directly with their offer terms, including requests for free shipping; I generally just ignore these messages or reply telling them that I only negotiate on items that have the *Best Offer* option on them.

Do not let potential customers bully you into selling your items for less. Buyers who send direct messages asking for a discount usually do so because they know that the item is indeed worth what you have listed it for, and they are trying to snatch it away before another buyer comes along. Or if you have the item up for *Auction*, they know that it will have multiple bidders and are trying to get you to sell it to them outright, so they do not have to compete in a bidding war.

Offers To Watchers: A fairly recent feature to Ebay's site is sellers' ability to send offers to interested customers. When someone "watches" an Ebay item, Ebay allows the seller to send an offer. You can choose a percentage or a set amount of the item's price, and the customer has 48-hours to accept. You can also enable the customer to submit a counteroffer. Sellers do not see the user name of the person they send the offer to.

For me, *Offers To Watchers* has proven to be the most effective way to generate a sale. It has worked better for me than either allowing buyers to submit offers to me or running sales in my store. I typically send offers out once or twice a week. Ebay makes sending offers incredibly easy. When you access your *Active Listings* in your *Seller Hub*, you will see a highlighted **Send offers – eligible** button highlighted above your listings. Clicking on this will take you to a new page where you can see all of the items that currently have watchers. You can choose to send offers through each individual listing, or you can send offers on all of the items by bulk selecting all of the listings, clicking on the **Send Offer** button, and choosing your terms. You can choose to offer a percentage off or a dollar amount off. You can add in a personalized message, although Ebay provides an automated "Here's your chance to get this item at a great price!" option. And you can also allow counteroffers from those who you send offers to.

Buyers have 48 hours to either decline or accept offers; although they can, and often do, just ignore them. And while many customers do not respond to offers, they may not be interested in purchasing your item but are instead either watching it as they plan to sell a similar item or are just curious to sell what it eventually sells for. So, don't be discouraged if you send out a number of offers and get no response. I still get enough of a response from customers who are actually interested in purchasing the items that it is worth it to me to send out offers regularly.

Pricing: While I do a completed listing search for every item I list on Ebay to determine a price, I tend to stick to a few key price points: $9.99, $24.99, $49.99, and $99.99. I choose these amounts for two reasons: One, these were the price points Ebay used to charge different fees for back when I first started selling on their site, and while they no longer do this, it was this way for years, and I've yet to break the habit. Two, customers have been trained over time to look for prices ending in 99-cents. After all, aren't you more willing to buy something priced at $24.99 instead of $26.45? When a customer is making a choice between spending UNDER $25 or OVER $25, even if the difference is only pennies and the shipping is more expensive or slower, they are more likely to spend the price point under the threshold.

Sticking to these price points has worked well for me over the years. Of course, if I have done my research and found that an item is selling for a different amount, I will undoubtedly price it accordingly. And I will also accept offers or run sales for lesser amounts. These numbers are my base prices, not always my final prices.

Many sellers will price items at $9.97 or $24.98, hoping that their items will appear before $9.99 or $24.99 in Ebay searches. However, it is essential to remember that Ebay shows items based on the *total* price, including shipping. So, if your shipping is higher than the competition, your listing will still appear after other listings despite any difference in the price of the item itself.

For auctions, I generally will not start the bidding lower than $9.99 unless I know for sure that I have a very desirable item OR if I just want to move stale inventory. If you start your auction at 99-cents, do so only if you are using the auction to draw traffic to your other listings, you are trying to move old items, or if you are confident that a bidding war will ensue. Otherwise, don't be upset when your item only sells for 99-cents. Ebay is flooded with 99-cent items, so be careful not to devalue your items by getting them lumped into the 99-cent listings that permeate the site. Even upping your starting bid to $1.99 or $2.99 will help cover your fees if your item only sells for the opening bid. And you can always add a dollar or two to your shipping fee to act as a buffer. I have seen many successful sellers run 99-cent auctions with a $9.99 shipping charge to ensure that all fees are covered and that they actually make a small profit.

The bottom line is that you want to price your items at the amount you will be happy with. If you want at least $20 for something, don't start the auction at $5; start it at $19.99. I see so many new sellers lose money by pricing their items too low, both at *Auction* and *Fixed Price*. These sellers do not make as much money, and the item itself gets devalued across the board. Again, do your research to determine what your item goes for on average and price yours accordingly. You may realize that it is almost always best for you to list them at *Fixed Price* for the types of items you sell so you make exactly what the item is worth.

Immediate Payment: One way to protect yourself from customers clicking to buy your items but then not paying is to require *Immediate Payment*. This can obviously only be done on *Fixed Price* items, not *Auctions*, and not on *Best Offer*, either from a buyer sending you an offer or with you using *Offers To Watchers.* And it may not be practical for you if you are a seller that frequently sells multiple items in the same transaction as it prevents you from combining a customer's order. For instance, if you specialize in golf accessories, you may sell several items in one transaction to the same customer; and sending them an invoice with combined shipping is essential.

However, if you are like me and sell mostly unique, individual items, requiring *Immediate Payment* can save you the hassle of dealing with non-paying buyers. The option to require *Immediate Payment* is available under the *Payment* section of all Ebay listings. I tend to be somewhat flexible on putting *Immediate Payment* on my listings by only using it for high-priced items. For small items under $10, I generally do not have *Immediate Payment* turned on as these are the items that are more likely to be purchased in multiples by the same customer. While one person may buy three $10 coffee mugs from me, it is rare that a single customer will come along and purchase three $100 silverware sets from my store simultaneously.

Discounts: You can set up automatic shipping discounts for customers who buy multiple items, either giving them a percentage or dollar-off discount or automatically providing free shipping when they spend a certain amount of money. This works best if all of your items tend to be the same size and weight; for instance, if you sell CDs or miniatures. It is much easier to estimate shipping costs when all of your products weigh roughly the same amount.

For example, you may set your shipping discounts to give customers free shipping when buying three or more items. Or you may give them $1 off for every item they buy after the first one. So, if they buy three $5 items, they will pay $5 for the first, and then $4 each for the other two.

If you have an **Ebay Store**, you can set up these types of automatic discounts using the **Promotions Manager** under the **Marketing Tab** in **Seller Hub.** For items to be eligible for *Promotions*, the listing must be in a *Fixed Price* format with *Buy It Now* pricing. Items will appear at the advertised price, and the discount will be applied to the buyer's shopping cart. You can offer five different types of offers using *Promotions Manager*:

- **Order discounts:** Offer discounts based on order size or the amount spent by a buyer. You can also create promotions such as a percentage off an additional item or a buy-one-get-one-free offer.
- **Codeless coupons:** Offer exclusive discounts to buyer groups of your choosing by using a virtual coupon.
- **Promotional shipping:** Offer cheaper shipping on items that qualify for your offer.
- **Sales events:** Reduce prices for selected items or categories.
- **Volume price discounts:** Offer tiered discounts to buyers who purchase multiple quantities of a single item.

I will discuss using promotions on Ebay more in-depth later in this book

Category: Before you even get to the pricing section of an Ebay listing, you will need to fill out several other fields, the first being the category of the item you are selling. There are hundreds of Ebay categories and subcategories to choose from, and narrowing down which to list each individual item in can be overwhelming.

Many categories are obvious. If you are selling a cookbook, you will choose the *Books* category and then the *Cookbooks* subcategory. However, for items you are unsure of, type a general description of the item into the search field to see what turns up. Ebay will show you a list of available categories, the first one being the most commonly used. While the first option is usually the one you will end up going with, be sure to look over the other choices to see if one is a better fit for your specific item.

You can also look at the categories similar items have sold in. Simply do a *Sold Completed Listing* search and open a few of the highest-priced sales to see which categories they were listed in and follow suit.

Ebay gives you the first category for free, but you can pay to have your item listed in a second category. Never once in all of my years selling on Ebay have I ever paid to have an item listed in a second category, and I recommend you don't, either. One category selection is all you need as it is not just the category but the title, photos, description, and shipping that help your item be found when customers are using Ebay's search tool. As you grow your Ebay business, it is important that you save on fees as much as possible so that more money ends up in your pocket, not in Ebay's hands!

Listing Title: More important than the category you list your item in, however, is the listing title itself. The title of your Ebay listing is what search engines use when customers search for items on either Ebay or via an internet search tool such as Google or Internet Explorer. A poorly worded title may not even get picked up in the search results, but a keyword-loaded title will bring in the maximum number of views, which in turn gives your item the best chance of actually selling.

When writing a title for your Ebay listing, it is important to remember that you do not need to write a perfectly structured sentence. Instead, you want to load up all of the available space with keywords that will not only be picked up in Ebay's search but also by internet search engines. Keywords are the key when filling out your listing's title field, so add in all the words you can, putting the most important words first.

For example, if you are selling a Ralph Lauren shirt, you don't want to simply put "Ralph Lauren Shirt" as your title. Instead, you want to load the space up with keywords by writing something like "Red Mens Polo RALPH LAUREN Dress Shirt LARGE Pony Logo Stretch." Note that the title does not read like a sentence but rather focuses on keywords that buyers are likely to type into the search engines.

I like to write my titles with the first letter of each word capitalized. "Red Ralph Lauren Mens Shirt" looks a lot better and more professional than "red ralph lauren mens shirt" or even "Red Ralph Lauren mens shirt," doesn't it?

Please do not waste space on silly words or phrases such as "L@@K" or "Open Now!" which bring in zero traffic and are often ignored by experienced shoppers. Pull every single searchable keyword you can think of, including color, material, size, country of origin if vintage, and/or unique features from the item you are selling, and cram those words into the title as those are the words buyers will be typing into the Ebay *Search* bar.

Just as you can pay to list your item in a second category, you can also pay extra to include a *Subtitle*. Again, just as I never pay for a second category, I never pay for subtitles. Ebay offers plenty of space in the title section to load it up with keywords; there is no need to spend money on a subtitle that most buyers will not even look at.

You also want to avoid punctuation in your titles. Notice how in the above example how I wrote "Mens" instead of "Men's"?

Punctuation not only takes up valuable space that could be used for additional keywords, but punctuation can also interfere with search results; it can mess up the entire word depending on what browser or computer the customer is using, making the words appear as a collection of characters (i.e., *!&#^) rather than letters.

When writing anything online, including your Ebay title, it is also important to not type in all capital letters. Tying in all caps is the online equivalent of yelling, so you want to avoid it as it is very off-putting for the reader. Capitalizing the most important words helps the title stand out; putting all of the letters in capitals would make it distracting and even unreadable to some customers.

For example, "Red Mens Polo RALPH LAUREN Dress Shirt LARGE Pony Logo Stretch" has three words in all caps while the rest of the words only have their first letters capitalized. The essential words pop out at the buyer, drawing them into the listing. However, when the title is in all caps, i.e., "RED MENS POLO RALPH LAUREN DRESS SHIRT LARGE PONY LOGO STRETCH," it is hard for the eye to pick out any works as the type pretty much runs together, thus turning off potential customers.

Loading up the main title field with keywords, capitalizing the first letter of every word, avoiding punctuation, and capitalizing two or three main keywords all are quick and easy tricks that will go a long way towards selling your item fast and for top dollar!

Item Specifics: Ebay provides a space for writing your own listing description as well as fields to fill in for item specifics. The listing specifics fields vary depending on what category you are listing in; clothing usually has many details you can provide (brand, size, fabric, color), while other categories may only have a couple of choices.

Ebay recently increased the number of *Item Specific* fields and categorized them into two sections within your listings: **Required** and **Suggested.** You HAVE to fill out all of the *Required* fields, but it is important to fill in all of the *Suggested* item specific fields that you can as these are used by customers to narrow down the search results. Buyers can choose clothing results by pattern and theme, for instance, so if you have a striped shirt, be sure to select "striped" in order for your listing to be better found in the search results.

For very crowded categories such as clothing, the *Item Specifics* can make or break a sale as they are crucial to helping customers find your listings. However, it is the clothing categories that Ebay has added the largest number of additional item specific fields to. Again, focus on the *Required* fields, and then enter in as many of the *Suggested* as you can. I don't stress about filling in too many of *Suggested* fields, and sometimes I find that they don't even relate to the item I am listing. These fields are continually being tweaked by Ebay, too, so they may vary from listing to listing. I just choose as many as I can and move on to completing my listing so that my item is available for sale.

Filling in these fields correctly not only goes a long way towards describing the items you are selling, but this information also protects you in case of customer complaints. Perhaps a customer says they thought the shirt they were buying was made of cotton, not wool. However, if you selected "cotton" in the item specifics, which will prove to Ebay that you accurately described the product. This is also why choosing too many *Suggested* specifics can backfire as you may accidentally choose an incorrect one. Hence, it is best to make sure your *Required* fields are all accurate and not worry too much about all of the *Suggested* options.

While you want to fill in as many *Item Specifics* as you can, I also recommend you put those same details in the actual item *Description*, too. While it is easy to assume customers will look at the *Item Specific* fields, some buyers skip over them and only look at the listing *Description*. On the other hand, some customers may only look at the *Item Specific* fields. To cut down on potential buyer questions, include the information in both sections.

Item Description: In the *Item Description* box, you want to not only include everything you provided in the *Item Specifics* fields, but you want to really try to "sell" your item by including something like "This stylish jacket will work on its own or layered with a tee-shirt!" or "This hard-to-find piece is a must for any collector!" There are hundreds of thousands of listings on Ebay at any one time, and you want to make sure your listing stands out from the competition.

I like to center my item description lines with space in between them. I "bold" the text and use size 14 Ariel font. I also only use black for the font color. And at the bottom of the listing, I used to put my Terms of Service. Over the years, my TOS changed a lot; and I no longer include it in my listings, relying instead on the settings Ebay provides in terms of payments and returns. However, below is what I used for years. I am showing you this version as it includes the instructions for returns. And while I am currently not accepting returns, I did for years.

PAYMENT: Payment is due via PayPal within two days.

DAMAGES & RETURNS: Any damages must be reported to us within 30 days of receiving your package. A photo of the damage is required to qualify for a refund. If you want to return an item, you must contact us within 14 days of receiving your order. Refunds will be issued once we have the item back in the same condition in which we originally shipped it. Return postage is the responsibility of the customer. We cannot refund the original cost of postage.

SHIPPING INFORMATION FOR U.S. CUSTOMERS: We work hard to offer our customers the lowest possible shipping price. We offer Media Mail for books and other media that qualify for this service, but please note that Media Mail can take a very long time to arrive. We ship via First Class for packages 16-ounces or less. We then offer Parcel Select and Priority Mail for packages weighing over 1 pound. We ship within two business days (i.e., weekday, not on weekends, or holidays) after payment has cleared.

SHIPPING INFORMATION FOR INTERNATIONAL CUSTOMERS: We now ship all international orders via Ebay's Global Shipping program.

I see so many listings where sellers take up most of the description space "threatening" potential buyers with statements like, "You must pay, or else I will report you!" or "Don't bid unless you want the item!". While it can be tempting to "put your foot down," so to speak, these statements will turn customers away and can even invite trouble. When I included a *Terms of Service* in my listings, it was at the very bottom of each listing and in a smaller font. I kept my actual listing verbiage upbeat and positive. After all, you wouldn't want a clerk "yelling" at you when you enter a brick-and-mortar store; so, treat potential Ebay customers with care. Ebay provides protections for both sellers and buyers that help ensure transactions go smoothly, and problems are dealt with fairly.

Details: Some Ebay categories require much more than just stating what the item is and providing a general description. When I list a vintage book, I copy all of the information on the title page (title, author, editor, publishing house, year), provide the number of pages, and measure its length and width. When I sell vintage hymnals, I put the number of pages and the number of songs (sometimes a hymnal will have 300 pages but contain 500 songs as some songs are so short that two to three can fit on the same page).

In fact, just as I do with books, simply copying what is on the outside of a box or the bottom of an electronic is the best and fastest way to describe items in more detail accurately. Instead of listing a vintage clock radio only by what brand it is, turn it over and copy whatever is on the bottom (country of manufacture, watts) into your listing. Even if the words make no sense to you (I honestly don't know what the number of Watts or Volts means!), a buyer who is explicitly searching for the product you are selling will understand. And providing these details up front will cut down on questions from potential customers as everything they need to know is already in the listing.

For clothing, you will need to provide measurements. A size "large" shirt in one brand often measures completely different in another. To measure shirts and jackets, I lay the garment on a flat surface. I then take three measurements, all in inches: across-the-chest (tape measure drawn from under one armpit across to the other), sleeve (tape measure drawn from the shoulder seam to the cuff; if there is no shoulder seam, I measure from the collar to the cuff, noting this in this listing); and body length (tape measure drawn from the top of the inside collar seam down to the hem).

For pants and skirts, I also lay the garment on a flat surface and measure the waist (tape measure drawn from one side of the waist to the other). I give an inseam measurement for pants (tape measure drawn from the crotch to the hem); for skirts and dresses, I give a length measurement (tape measure drawn from waist to hem).

In addition to providing the clothing measurements, I also explain HOW I took the measurements. Is this all a lot of extra work? Yes. But it serves two significant purposes. Number one is that it dramatically reduces customer questions as I provide ALL information in the listing. And number two is that it significantly reduces the number of returns. In fact, it is very rare anyone returns a piece of clothing to me because it did not fit because if it didn't fit, it is the buyer who is to blame for not checking the measurements.

Details, details, details; it's all in the details when it comes to creating Ebay listings. Taking the time to include every single detail about the item you are selling into the listing will help you get top dollar and result in a happy customer. And happy customers leave positive feedback and continue to shop on the Ebay site!

Relist vs. Sell Similar: When relisting an item, don't automatically choose the **Relist** option; a better choice is actually **Sell Similar.** When you simply *Relist* an item, it gets put back onto the Ebay site with its original item number, which says to Ebay that it is an item that has been on the site for a while. However, when you choose *Sell Similar*, the item specifics will remain the same, but the listing will get a new Ebay item number and be put into the Ebay search engine as a newly listed item.

With so many items for sale on Ebay, one way Ebay keeps listings fresh for buyers is to give priority to newly listed items. Selecting *Relist* will just get your item buried further down in the search results as Ebay will see it as something that has been on the site for a long time. However, *Sell Similar* makes it a brand-new listing that will be put into the **Newly Listed** search.

The exception to choosing *Relist* over *Sell Similar* would be if the item that has ended had a lot of watchers and had gotten a lot of traffic. If that is the case, you may want to stick with *Relist* so that those buyers will still have it on their watch lists. If I have an item that hasn't sold in 30 days and doesn't have any watchers, I will end the listing and then use the *Sell Similar* feature to relist it; however, if the item has a few watchers, I may still end it, but I will use the *Relist* option so that the person who has been watching it will still have it in their "watch" list. Or I may let that listing go for another month to see if any of those watchers end up buying it.

The decision to end listings used to be easier when you could list *Fixed Price* items for one, three, five, seven, ten, or thirty days. Now, however, Ebay lists all *Fixed Price* items as *Good 'Till Cancelled.* I have found it beneficial to manually end listings after 30 days to give them a "reset" in the system. However, that is something you will have to decide is or isn't beneficial for you.

If you choose to manually end your items and then use the *Sell Similar* option to relist them, it is a great time to give your listing another look to examine why it hasn't sold. Your title may need to be reworked to add in more keywords. Perhaps you could redo some photos or add in better measurements. There may be more information you can include, such as filling in more *Item Specific* fields or adding more details into the *Description.* Or you may consider adjusting the price, adding *Best Offer*, or adding in a free shipping option. Just because an item ended its initial run without selling doesn't mean that there aren't things you can do to improve the listing to sell the next time around!

Creating a New Listing: When I have a new item to list, instead of listing it from scratch, I simply open up an *Active* listing and click on the **Sell a similar item** option in the top left corner. I then change the category (if needed), title, photos, item specifics, description field, and shipping weight; however, all of my other settings, such as my shipping and return policies, remain in place.

Creating a new listing off of an active one makes the listing process go a lot faster as I don't have to reset my policies and requirements every single time I list a new item. I often list several like-items in a row, such as coffee mugs, Bibles, or clothing. This allows me to keep a lot of the information in the description field the same; I just change each piece's specifics. For instance, if I am listing coffee mugs that are all the same brand and size but have different patterns, the only changes in the new listing I will need to make are changing the pattern in the title, item specifics, and description field, as well as adding in the new photos. Everything else, such as the brand, measurements, and materials, remain the same.

If you use this *Sell Similar* trick, make sure to change all relevant information. I have been careless at times and overlooked writing a new title, for instance! I have also accidentally left the "free shipping" option checked for an item I expected the customer to pay the shipping on. While using the *Sell Similar* feature is fast and easy, it can also make you lazy, so be sure to look over your listing carefully after it goes live to make sure all of the information and settings are correct.

Full Disclosure: It is important to be completely honest in your

Ebay listings. Customers are taking you at your word that an item is as you state; if they find a flaw or error that you did not disclose, it will come back to you in the form of an unhappy buyer, a return, and/or negative feedback.

Since most items sold on Ebay are secondhand, you must look over the pieces you are selling very carefully to find flaws. Even a small mark that you doubt anyone else will see should be disclosed within the listing, both under the *Condition* section as well as in the *Item Description* field. Don't list an item as "MINT" when it, in fact, was found on the floor of a thrift store. "MINT" and "BRAND NEW" both indicate that the item's condition is exactly this same as it was when it initially rolled off the assembly line. I usually understate the condition of my items. If I have something in excellent condition, I list it as great. If it is great, I list it as good.

If I buy an item at an estate sale and know for sure that the original owner was a non-smoker, I will state, "From a clean, smoke-free home!" in the listing. I wash all ceramics, and I also wash clothes in non-scented detergent because many people are sensitive to fragrances. I have had several customers over the years message me to specifically request that I do not put a dryer sheet in their package, for instance, as this is a trick some sellers use to make items appear cleaner. I do everything I can to make sure that items are as clean as possible so that they show up nicely in photos and when they arrive at the customer's home.

The best piece of advice I ever got when I started selling on Ebay was to **under-promise and over-deliver.** I try to understate the condition of items a bit so that buyers don't have unrealistic expectations. I often receive positive feedback that reads, "Better than expected" or "In much better condition than I was expecting."

Photos: While an excellent tile and description are fundamental when selling on Ebay, neither is enough to ensure a sale. Just as important (and in some cases even more so) are your product photos. Great pictures not only attract customers to your listings, but accurate photos help protect you as buyers know exactly what they are purchasing.

You don't have to be an expert photographer or have the most expensive camera equipment to take great Ebay photos. The following tips and tricks will help you quickly and easily take pictures that will result in Ebay sales.

Item Pictures: Ebay allows sellers to add up to 12 photos per listing, and you should take full advantage of that and provide as many pictures as possible of the item you are selling. Take photos of the piece from every single angle, including from the top and the bottom. You want to give your customers the feeling they would have if they were in a brick-and-mortar store handling an item. You likely don't purchase something by only glancing at it briefly on the shelf, so you will sell more on Ebay if you give your customers pictures of your items from every angle.

If you are selling a coffee mug, for instance, take pictures of the front, back, both sides, bottom, along with a shot of the inside (customers want to see if there are any "spoon marks," i.e., scratches or discoloration). For clothes, take full-length shots of the garment's front and back and up-close pictures of hems, cuffs, pockets, and labels. If your item is battery-powered, take a photo of the open battery compartment to show that there isn't any erosion. When I list vintage books, I take photos of the front and back cover, the spine, the first couple of title pages, and two to three photos of the text pages.

You want the item you are selling to be front and center in all pictures, so take the time to edit your photos to eliminate as much white space as possible. Most computers come with easy-to-use built-in photo editing software; I use a PC and have Picasa, which came with my system and is powered by Google.

However, I currently take all of my Ebay photos with my iPhone. They are automatically saved to my camera roll, and I can edit them right on my phone before uploading them to Ebay. Some resellers go a step further and using photo editing apps to enhance their pictures; Photoshop and Canva are two popular options.

Ebay recently added the ability to remove your photos' background and turn the space to pure white. However, this is a new feature and has proven not to work very well with most items, sometimes cutting entire parts of the item itself out. I don't worry about my pictures looking perfect; I focus on making sure my photo area is well lit and that it is against a white background (such as a wall or piece of posterboard). I worry more about making sure my pictures are clear with the item in focus than I do the background.

When I am taking pictures of items to list on Ebay, I make sure to take up-close photos of any condition issues such as minor wear or damage. I disclose any faults in the listing, and I also direct buyers to look closely at the photos provided, so they know exactly what they are buying. It is rare to find secondhand items that do not have even a tiny bit of wear and tear. Still, by disclosing all issues and providing photos, you will not only have a better chance of the item selling, but you will also protect yourself from a customer complaining they received something that was not as described. Buyers understand that they are purchasing pre-owned items and don't expect them to be perfect, but they rightly do expect that the seller provides them with an accurate condition.

It is important to take up-close pictures of details such as the maker's marks on ceramics, clothing labels (both the size label by the collar as well as fabric labels that may be located elsewhere, such as near the inside hem), and any inscriptions, as well as any condition issues. The cameras on most of today's smartphones take pictures that are just as good and sometimes even better than actual digital cameras. In particular, my iPhone is much better at capturing up-close details than the digital camera I used to use ever.

After taking my pictures on my iPhone and editing them in my camera roll, I open up the Ebay app, click on one of my active listings, and then click on the *Sell Similar* option. Ebay automatically asks if I want to keep or remove the photos from that listing; I select "remove" and then upload the photos I just took directly from my camera roll. I then saved that listing as a *Draft* and switched over to my laptop to complete the listing. Some Ebay sellers complete the entire listing process on their smartphones via the Ebay app; I just personally find it easier to finish listings on my computer, mainly because I sell so many different items with different shipping weights.

Note that you want the item's main photo, the one that will appear as the **Thumbnail** in the Ebay search results, to be the photo that shows your entire item. For instance, if you are selling a coffee mug, you want the mug's front to be the main thumbnail picture. Sometimes when I upload my photos from my phone into an Ebay listing, the photos upload out of order. This is yet another reason why I like to finish listings on my computer as it is easier to correct such details. Ensure all photos are upright, not sideways or upside down, and do not upload blurry photos. I cannot tell you how many lousy item photos I see on Ebay, and poor-quality pictures can make it next to impossible for an item to sell. It is better to retake photos than upload poor ones.

Lighting: You do not need a fancy photography set-up to take Ebay photos, just a space with a lot of light. Good lighting is essential to taking clear pictures that capture color and detail, along with any flaws.

If your home or workspace is dark, you can easily brighten things up with lamps. If you are frequently listing many items online, you may want to invest in some professional lighting, such as a **ring lamp,** although I never found this necessary. However, if you are listing many like items, such as clothing, you may find a professional lighting set up to be beneficial. If you rely on natural light for your photos, a lighting set up will allow you to list even on gloomy days. Ring light systems can be purchased online for as little as $50.

A **lightbox** is a tool that sellers of small items such as jewelry and miniatures like to use. Portable lightboxes can be purchased for around $50 online, although there are all sorts of YouTube tutorials on making your own using cardboard boxes and lights. I own a lightbox, but I rarely get it out for photos. I find that these sorts of extra listing tools work best if you can leave them up permanently. Because I have to get mine out and then put it away every time I want to use it, I find myself not bothering with it.

I take my Ebay photos in a room with lots of windows that provide ample natural lighting. I also turn all of the room's lights, as well as a lamp, to add more brightness. I want to make sure to capture the actual color and texture of the items I am selling. Rarely do I use my camera flash, which often distorts the product's actual color, making it appear lighter than it is. My iPhone has some editing features for the light that I occasionally use, especially if an item's color does not show up correctly (this usually happens to me with anything green).

Backdrops: I see so many Ebay sellers who take pictures of items on their dirty carpet or with their messy kitchen in the background. I have even seen pictures of packaged food products taken on the floor with a pet's tail in the shot!

Taking pictures against a white background will work for most items, whether it is a white wall, a sheet, or a table. I have a very simple set up of white poster boards for my photos. I set one on a table and the other against a wall to form a slight angle. I buy the boards at the dollar store for $1 each, and I also have a set in black for light-colored items that do not show up against a white background.

For larger items, it is easy to take pictures against a white wall. If you do not have a white wall, draping a white sheet from the ceiling can provide a nice backdrop. I have a blank white wall in my office with a single nail that I hang clothes from to take photos.

You want to make sure that whatever backdrop you use is clean and pattern-free so that nothing takes away from the item itself.

Whatever you use as your backdrop, just make sure that the item you are selling is the only item in the picture. I cannot tell you how many photos I see where other things and even people and pets are in the photos. Make sure to edit your hands/fingers out of pictures. I occasionally need to hold down a book page to get a photo, but I always edit my hand out. Unless you are a hand model, no one wants to see your chipped nails and cracked cuticles. Yuck!

Stock Photos: If you sell an item with a bar code in Ebay's catalog, a stock photo will often pop up to use as the main picture in your listing. And while many sellers use these photos, I do not like them, preferring to use my pictures. Sometimes I use Ebay's provided stock photo, but not as the main picture; I keep it in the listing and have it at the end of my photo lineup.

Stock photos indicate the item is brand new, and even if you have a new, unused item to sell, you likely picked it up secondhand. There may be differences in the item you are selling versus the products' original stock photo, including slight damage. And unless an item is brand new and in Ebay's catalog with the photo they provide or you have obtained permission from the manufacturer, wholesale, or liquidation company that the item came from to use their photos, it is unethical to use stock photos.

In some cases, it is even illegal to use a company's stock photo without their permission. If you are purchasing items via wholesale or liquidation and those companies provide you with stock photos, you will still need permission to use those pictures on Ebay. Do not go directly to a company's website and copy their pictures for your Ebay listing; not only will that get you into trouble with Ebay, but it could also result in legal action from the business whose photos you stole.

Even if I am selling matches the approved stock pictures exactly,

I still take my own photos as I feel they best represent my specific products. While customers turn to Amazon to buy brand new items, they often come to Ebay looking for gently used products or extreme deals. So, while it is reasonable to expect an Amazon listing with an available quantity of one hundred products to use stock photos, on Ebay, most people are just selling one single version of each of the items they have listed. And by providing photos of the exact item you are selling, you assure customers that what they see in the picture is exactly what they are getting.

While you will likely see other sellers using stock photos on Ebay, please remember that just because some people are getting away with it does not mean you should, too. Do you really want to risk losing your Ebay account because you didn't want to take a few pictures? I know I don't!

CHAPTER THREE: PROMOTION & MARKETING

When I first started selling online, Ebay and Amazon were the only two e-commerce retailers. Customers who shopped online only had those two sites to choose from, so there was no need for sellers to seek out buyers. However, nowadays, it is often not enough to simply list an item on Ebay for it to sell; you now have to do some promotion and marketing to drive sales, both on the Ebay site directly as well as on social media platforms in order to compete with the thousands of other e-commerce sites out there.

Fortunately, most of these promotional tools are free and easy to use, especially when it comes to utilizing social media sites to promote your Ebay listings. By adding some or all of the following marketing methods, you will see your Ebay traffic and sales increase. In some cases, you may need to spend a little bit of money (such as if you decide to set up a website and/or have enclosures printed up); but even then, the costs are still relatively low compared to the huge differences these efforts can make for your sales.

Blog/Website: If Ebay is your part-time or full-time business, it may be worth it to you to set up a blog or even a full-fledged website to further connect with customers. If you are going to have a site, however, be sure to commit to maintaining it. Nothing is worse than going to someone's blog and seeing that they haven't updated it in months.

However, if you are only selling on Ebay occasionally or just for a bit of extra money, then you do not need to burden yourself with the work of maintaining a site. Ask yourself the following questions:

- Do you plan to write lengthy articles discussing the items you sell?
- Are you looking to use your site not just as a sales channel but also as a teaching tool?
- Would you like to sell products directly from your website outside of Ebay, or are you selling your items on other online sites (Amazon, Etsy) and/or at brick-and-mortar retail locations (your own shop or at an antique mall)?
- Would you like to explore affiliate advertising and/or sell advertising to earn extra money for your site?

If you answered "yes" to any of the above questions, then you may want to consider starting a site. However, you will need to decide whether to go with a free blogging platform or a paid website. If you decide to go the paid route, you can invest in a sophisticated system or choose a simple, low-cost one. Yes, there are lots of decisions to make!

In addition to selling on Ebay, I also have a blog at AnnEckhart.com. I use my blog to promote my books and YouTube videos, many of which are devoted to teaching people how to make money on Ebay. Before I started my current blog, I had dabbled in blogging a few different times on Blogger, which is Google's blog platform. I had a blog dedicated solely to Ebay. However, when I started AnnEckhart.com, I closed that blog and moved all content to my new website.

The difference between that Ebay blog and my current blog is that my Ebay blog was just a blog, whereas my AnnEckhart.com blog is technically a website that hosts my blog. So, I now have a blog ON a website.

Huh? A blog ON a website? Confused? Don't worry, I was, and still am sometimes, confused! Even today, I struggle with whether to call AnnEckhart.com a blog or a website. In the beginning, I called it a website, but these days I call it a blog, even though it is actually a website, mainly because the term "blog" is more prevalent in the social media world. Oy!

To put it simply, a blog that is on a free site such as Blogger or WordPress is just a blog. However, a website is a site that you own that utilizes blogging software. AnnEckhart.com is my website, and on my website, I use WordPress blogging software. When you have a blog on a free site, it is actually not yours but instead belongs to the company behind the site you are using. It could be shut down at any time, and you would then lose all of your content. And while Blogger and WordPress have been around for years and show no signs of going anywhere, the risks are still there that you could eventually lose all of your content.

When I had my Ebay blog on Blogger, I didn't put anything significant on it; I just posted about new listings and had the links to my social networking sites. I rarely even promoted the blog; I just maintained it so that if anyone happened to stumble across it, they would hopefully click through to my Ebay store.

However, my current blog is actually a business for me as I earn income through affiliate advertising. I also load it with a lot of original content. If it were on a free blogging site, all of that information could be lost at a moment's notice. However, as long as I keep paying my website maintenance fees, my content is safe.

If you are looking for another way to drive traffic to your Ebay listings, stick with creating a simple free blog that links to your Ebay store and your other social networking sites. Try to update it a couple of times a week with a brief description of new listings or any sales you are running. Pictures are essential, too.

Both Blogger and WordPress offer free blogging platforms. Note, however, that Google owns blogger; therefore, you can apply for a Google AdSense account and place ads on your blog. So not only will you be helping drive traffic to your Ebay listings to increase sales, but you will also be able to earn advertising revenue. Note that while I utilize WordPress blogging software on my website and have affiliate advertising on it, the FREE WordPress blog does not allow much in the way of advertising options. So, if you would like a free blog that allows ads, go with Blogger.

However, if you decide to go with a paid website, do your research as there are a lot out there to choose from. I went with a large company (Bluehost.com) because I wanted my blog to be the centerpiece of my brand and because I wanted to utilize several forms of affiliate advertising on it. If your main business is selling on Ebay, you want your *Ebay Store* to be your brand, with your blog/website acting as an additional tool to drive traffic to your listings. There a lot of low-cost website options out there. For instance, you can not only register for the website URL's on GoDaddy.com, but they also offer website inexpensive hosting and simple websites.

As I said, my blog is an actual business, a company that I earn an income from. While I share Ebay information on my site, I also share recipes, reviews, and sponsored content. In addition to writing books like this one about Ebay, I also make YouTube videos about how I make money on Ebay. I share my books and videos on my blog, so all three (blog, YouTube, books) work together to promote each other.

So, which should you choose? A free blog or a website? Or no site at all? That is a decision only you can make. Having a blog or website for your Ebay business is NOT a requirement. In fact, it may actually be more work than is worth it for you. And as I will talk about later in this chapter, you may find that a Facebook page can just as easily act as your "website."

However, if you do decide to set up an Ebay blog or website, it doesn't have to be complicated. Think of it as the "home" page for your business where you provide the link to your Ebay store as well as the links to all of your other social networking sites (Facebook, Twitter, Pinterest, etc., which I'll discuss further in this chapter).

If you sell on other websites in addition to Ebay, a blog/website is a great place to provide the links to those places (Amazon, Etsy, flea markets, and/or antique malls). In addition to posting about new inventory and sales, you can include photos and talk about what is going on behind-the-scenes with your business. Having a site gives people a more personal look as to who you are. Also, it confirms that you are running a legitimate business, both of which can go a long way towards building up trust and reassuring people that they can buy from you with confidence.

Note that in addition to posting updates on your blog that you will need to maintain it. If you allow visitors to leave comments on your posts, you will want to make sure to respond to them. You also want to make sure all links are active and up-to-date so that people don't click through and get an error.

Suppose you are selling a significant number of items on Ebay and plan to continue with it as your primary business. In that case, you may want to register for a domain name, i.e. a personal website address that matches your Ebay Store name. For years, I have maintained a URL of my Ebay Store name that sends people directly to my Ebay Store. Having a URL gives you an easy web address to share with customers that is shorter and easier to remember than the long store URL you would otherwise have to promote (i.e. http://stores.ebay.com/yourebaystorename). You can purchase domain names on a website like GoDaddy.com.

You will also have to decide *where* you want the URL to direct users to. Do you want people to go to your blog FIRST, or do you want them to always go to your Ebay Store? Remember, you should be using a blog/website to *compliment* your Ebay Store, not as a replacement. If you decide to go with a free blog on a site like Blogger, you may want to choose a URL that sends people directly to your Ebay Store (i.e., www.MyStore.com) and keep the URL you get from Blogger for your website as-is. Or choose another URL such as MyEbayStoreBlog.com just for your site.

My advice is to have a personalized URL address that points to your Ebay store as getting Ebay sales should always be your first priority. Your website should work to direct traffic to your Ebay listings, not to intercept them.

Enclosures: When I first started selling on Ebay in 2005, I was adamant that I wouldn't include a packing slip in my shipments. After all, why should I spend more money on ink and paper for something that most customers would likely just throw away?

Fortunately, more experienced Ebay sellers counseled me on the importance of including a packing slip with all orders. After all, I expect a packing slip in MY packages when I place an order online. I am always put off when I open a box only to find the item I ordered inside but with no packing slip or enclosure of any kind. "Do on To Others" definitely holds true when it comes to putting packing slips into your Ebay packages! Now I can't imagine NOT including a packing slip inside all of my outgoing orders, and I encourage all sellers to include them.

Ebay makes including a packing slip incredibly easy. After you print a shipping label, a screen comes up with the option to **Print a Packing Slip**. Simply print it out, fold it up, and put it inside the box or envelope the item is being shipped out in.

I also like to include promotional enclosures in my packages that promote my Ebay store. In the past, I included either standard-size postcards or magnets from VistaPrint with my store logo on them. On the postcards, I thanked the customer for their order, provided them with the URL to my Ebay store, and gave the handle for my Ebay store's Facebook page. These days I put all of that information onto business-size cards; the business cards are cheaper than the postcards and magnets. However, it was more important for me to bring in repeat customers when I was selling gift items; now that I sell all different types of products, it's not as likely that buyers will continue to come back to my Ebay store as they likely found the item they purchased from me using an internet search or via Ebay's search, not by typing in my Ebay store URL.

Mailing List: When I sold new gift items, I tended to get a lot of repeat customers. I developed my own email mailing list using the PayPal email address that I had access to once someone paid me. I simply copied and pasted email addresses into a Word document and then put them into the *Blind Carbon Copy* section of my email program when I wanted to send out a message.

However, with Ebay's *Managed Payments*, sellers no longer have access to customer emails. If you sell a lot of similar items, you can always create your own mailing list using a service such as Constant Contact or Mail Chimp and letting customers know that they can sign up for the list in an enclosure card include in their order. Note that it is against Ebay's policy for you to use their messaging system to direct people off their site, so if you want to cultivate a mailing list, be sure to do so off the Ebay system.

Again, I would only consider a mailing list if you sell similar items. If like most resellers, you have a wide variety of different items for sale on Ebay, I would skip the mailing list and instead focus on creating listings that will show up high in internet search rankings (keyword loaded titles, good photos, and accurate descriptions.).

Facebook: If you plan to be selling a lot of items on Ebay, it is worth your time to set up a Facebook page to promote your listings. Some sellers choose to make their personal Facebook page their business page, too. Still, suppose you are already actively participating on Facebook by using your personal page to communicate with your friends and family. In that case, I recommend that you set up a separate business page. A personal page is one where people add you as a "friend," while a business page is one people must "like."

I prefer the business page format for promoting Ebay listings because it keeps your personal life and business separate. There is a limit to how many "friends" you can accept to a personal page, but you can grow an unlimited number of business "fans" on a business page. However, to start a business page, you need first to have a personal page.

To set up a Facebook business page, simply visit **facebook.com/ about/pages.** You will need to log into your personal Facebook account first, and then the system will walk you through the steps needed to create your business page. It is FREE and easy to set up.

The first decision you will need to make is to name your page. I currently have three Facebook business pages: one for my Ebay store, one for my own names (to promote my books and videos), and one for my stationery brand. If you are starting your Facebook page specifically for your Ebay business, then you'll want to make the names match.

In fact, as you go forward with creating more social media accounts related to your Ebay business, you will want to make sure they all have the same name. Now is the time to evaluate your Facebook user name to make sure it matches your Ebay store and is a good name overall. For instance, if you have been using the Ebay user name "i_luv_cats," you may want to change it to something more professional.

To change your Ebay username, simply go to **My eBay** and then **Account**. Click **Personal Information** on the left side of the page. Then click **Edit** to the right of the information you want to change.

To change the name of your Ebay Store, simply go to **My eBay,**

Account, and then **Subscriptions**. On the **Manage My Store: Summary** page, scroll to the **Set Up, Sell and Track** section, and click the **Design Your Store** link. In the **Display Settings** section, click the **Change** link and make your edits.

Once you have gotten your Ebay username and Ebay Store name's straight, you can proceed with naming your Facebook page the same.

There are all kinds of things you can personalize on your Facebook page. You can add a profile picture and a banner. I have my logo as my profile picture, and I had a custom banner made on Fiverr.com, although you can also design your own graphics using sites such as Canva and apps such as WordSwag. Whatever photos or graphics you choose, remember that this is your BUSINESS page, so keep it professional.

You will also want to fill out the extensive **About** section to provide people with information about your page and business. However, since this is your BUSINESS page and separate from your personal page, you want to be careful with how much information you provide. While you may share your cell phone number on your personal page so that friends and family can call or text you, unless you have a brick-and-mortar location that you actually want people to call, you'll want to leave that section blank on your business page.

You will first need to choose the **Category** for your page; as an Ebay seller, there are several you can choose from, such as "Companies & Organizations," "Local Businesses," or "Websites & Blogs." Any of the three would be sufficient for your Ebay page; it really up to you which you prefer. You will need to select a subcategory, too. And don't worry about being locked into your selections; you can easily change them at any time.

In addition to your **Name** (the name of your page, i.e., your Ebay business name), you can edit your Facebook URL so that it ends in that name. The URL for my Ebay store's Facebook page is https://

www.facebook.com/annabellasgs; as you can see, it ends with my Ebay store name.

The **About** section has fields for both a **Short Description** and a **Long Description**. I have my tagline in the *Short* section and a much more detailed account of what I do in the *Long* section.

Since you provided information about you and your business in the *Short* and *Long* description sections, use the **General Information** field to share the links to your other social media sites. You'll want to **put the address to your Ebay Store in the main Website field** (remember, your main goal is to drive traffic to your Ebay listings), but add any other links you may have (blog/website, Twitter, Pinterest, Instagram, etc.) to the *General Information* section so that users can easily connect with you on all of your social media platforms.

One great feature you can add to your Facebook page is a **Shop Now** tab that will take users directly to your Ebay Store. Simply click on **More** at the top of the page and select **Manage Tabs** to add a **Call to Action – Shop Now** button. Link it to your Ebay Store to create an easy way for your Facebook fans to shop your Ebay listings.

Finally, at the top of the page, click on **Settings** to determine how users can interact with you. I have stringent privacy settings for my page. I don't allow people to message me or post on my wall. When I had these two features turned off, I was inundated with messages and posts. However, if having messages from people is okay with you, then, by all means, leave those options open. You can always change them later on.

Once you have your page set up, it's time to start building your audience by getting people to "Like" your page. You'll be able to invite friends and family on your personal page to "Like" your new business page. If you are a part of Ebay groups, you can also post about your new page and hope that fellow Ebayers will support you.

In order to bring customers (past, present, or potential) to your Facebook page, include the link to your page on any package enclosures. I have business card sized "thank you" notes that go into every order printed with the direct link to my Ebay store as well as the links to my blog and social media accounts.

So, you've set up a Facebook page for your business and have started getting people to "Like" it. Now what? Providing useful content on your page will be vital to keeping it up to date and attracting new followers.

I share my newest listings directly to my Facebook page as Ebay makes this incredibly easy to do. In the upper right-hand corner of all active Ebay listings are **social media "Share" icons** for *Facebook, Twitter, Pinterest,* and *Email.* Simply click on the **Facebook icon**, change the page you want to post to (it will show you your personal page and business page, so be sure to select your business page), type in something like "Just Listed!" or "On Sale!", and then hit "Share." In only a few seconds, many of the people who have "Liked" your page will now have your listing on their Facebook feed!

In addition to sharing listings, it is also a good idea to engage your Facebook fans by posting status updates about what is going on with your business, such as if you are getting in new inventory or if you are running a sale. You want to keep your business page postings POSITIVE; stay away from religious, political, or other controversial topics. Remember, your goal with Ebay is to MAKE money, and you can't do that by offending people. Save the personal commentary for your personal Facebook page.

Posting pictures of your office, new inventory, or even a shot of orders ready to ship out are all fun ways to keep your audience interested. And sharing unique content is vital to ensure people actually SEE your posts.

Facebook makes it increasingly difficult for people to see all content on their feeds as Facebook wants page owners to purchase advertising. You may have noticed a little "Boost" link under your posts. "Boosting" a post means that you have to PAY for Facebook to show it to people. Pricing for this starts at $5; the more you pay, the more people Facebook will show your ad to.

If your sales are slow, it can be tempting to start boosting all of your posts in order to drive traffic to your Ebay listings. And while it can be advantageous to spend $5 here and there to help people see your content, don't let yourself become consumed if every post doesn't reach a wide audience. Likely, the links you share of your listings won't be shown to as many people as photos you post directly to your page (i.e., unique content).

I share the link to every blog post I write to my Facebook page, but it is the pictures I share directly to the page that get the most views and the most "Likes." Use this to your advantage by posting a new photo at least a few times a week to create engagement from your Facebook followers.

As I mentioned earlier, you may decide that a Facebook page can act like your blog or website rather than setting up a separate site. Many Ebay sellers do not have a blog or website, instead using Facebook as their homepage. So, unless you have the time to devote to maintaining a separate website, consider just using Facebook along with other social networking to promote your Ebay business. I recommend you do Facebook FIRST as you can always add a blog/website later on.

Facebook is just the first in a long list of social media sites you can create in conjunction with your Ebay business. Master your Facebook page first before moving on to the next social media account: Twitter!

Twitter: If you don't already have a Twitter account, you can create one for FREE at Twitter.com. If you do have an account that you are active on, consider creating a new one just for your Ebay business. As with Facebook, you want to keep your personal and business lives separate on Twitter. Make sure your Twitter handle is the same as your Ebay username, Ebay Store name, and Facebook business page name.

Twitter allows users to share posts of 140 characters or less. And just like Facebook, Twitter is a fast, easy, and free way to promote your listings. As with sharing your listings to Facebook, Ebay makes it easy to share your Twitter listings using the share button located in all active Ebay listings (in the upper right-hand corner).

To share a listing via Twitter, first, you will want to copy the title of your listing to your clipboard (simply highlight and select "copy"). Ebay and Twitter often have a generic "check out what I found on Ebay" title already in place when you click on the Twitter share button, so you will want to replace that with your keyword-loaded title. Simply delete the text in the Tweet that you want to replace and paste in your title.

Adding in hashtags is another easy way to make sure potential customers see your Tweet. A hashtag is a pound (#) sign followed by a keyword, and it is what experienced Twitter users enter into the search field to seek out relevant Tweets. For example, let's say you Ebay listing title is "Red Mens Polo RALPH LAUREN Dress Shirt LARGE Pony Logo Stretch." Put that into a new Twitter "tweet," followed by the link to the listing. And after the link, add in hashtags such as #RalphLauren #Polo #MensClothing.

Note that due to Twitter's 140 characters' restriction, you may need to cut down your listing title for it, the Ebay link, and your hashtags to all fit. You could easily drop the last three words (Pony Logo Stretch) from Twitter to make room in the above example. You want to keep the most relevant keywords, which in that case are "Red Mens Polo RALPH LAUREN Dress Shirt," followed by the link to the listing.

Just as you share your Facebook page with customers via a blog/website and/or package enclosures (as I've said, I include business card size "thank you" notes in all of my Ebay packages with my

Ebay store link as well as all of my social media URL's), you'll also want to share your Twitter handle with them in the hopes they will follow you on Twitter, too. And to find even more followers, you want to engage with other Twitter users actively.

Some Twitter users follow everyone who follows them, which can certainly help build up your followers. You can also "network" with other folks on Twitter by replying to, retweeting, or favoring tweets. As I mentioned when setting up your Facebook page, you can add all of your social media links, including your Twitter URL, in the "About" section; so hopefully, some of your Facebook fans will follow you to Twitter. To encourage this, about once a week, post your Twitter link directly to your Facebook page to make it easy for people to click through and "follow" you.

What you want to gain from Twitter is people clicking through to your Ebay listing links and either purchasing that item or finding something else to buy from you. You will also likely see that some people "favor" your Tweets by clicking on the little star icon under each message. It's always nice when someone retweets one of your Tweets, too, so that it gets shared with their followers.

Note that just as people can message you on Facebook (unless you change the privacy settings to block them), you can also send and receive messages on Twitter. And finally, you can create "Lists" on Twitter to group people you follow together (such as "customers," "Ebay sellers," "celebrities," "news," etc.).

Pinterest: Pinterest started as a way for people, mainly women, to "pin" craft ideas and recipes to virtual boards. However, Pinterest is quickly becoming a tool for businesses to get the word out about their products and develop brand loyalty. Pinterest offers Ebay sellers another fast and free way to promote their listings in the hopes that people will click through and purchase products.

As with Facebook and Twitter, Ebay provides a Pinterest "share" button in all active listings (in the upper right-hand corner). I have a "For Sale on Ebay" board on Pinterest that I "pin" my listings to. Not only can my Pinterest followers then see my new listings, but they can share the pin with THEIR Pinterest followers by pinning it to their own boards.

You will find lots of other Ebay sellers on Pinterest, many of whom have created Ebay group boards that you may be invited to post to. Networking with fellow Ebay sellers on Pinterest is another excellent way to promote your listings while getting to know other Ebayers such as yourself. Re-pinning THEIR pins is a nice gesture and a great way to network.

One concern many Ebay sellers have is that once items sell, the "pin" is no longer relevant. Should you delete old pins of items that have sold? While you certainly can take the time to do this, you don't have to. In fact, it may be beneficial for you to leave the pin active. Why? Well, let's say someone sees a pin of a collectible you have for sale. When they click through, they find that the item has sold. However, they are now connected with you on Ebay and may click on the link to visit your Ebay store or to see your current listings. While they may be annoyed that the item they wanted is no longer available, they also might find something else to buy from you.

Just as you should be doing with your Facebook and Twitter links, be sure to share your Pinterest page with customers by including the link on your blog/website (if you have one) and in the General Information section of your Facebook page. You can also provide the URL to your Pinterest account in any package enclosures. Be sure to periodically share your Pinterest link on both Facebook and Twitter in order to attract new followers.

You may be noticing by now that a big part of social networking is to have all of your sites working together. Include all of your social media links on your blog/website and in package enclosures.

Post your Twitter and Pinterest links to Facebook; share your Facebook and Pinterest links on Twitter. The more you can get your Ebay links out there, the easier it will be for customers to find you and for you to make more sales and make more money!

Instagram: Like Facebook, Twitter, and Pinterest, Instagram is easy and FREE to use! While Ebay doesn't yet provide a "share" button for Instagram, it is still a useful tool for promoting your listings. You can currently only add photos to your Instagram through their apps, so note that you will need to have a phone or tablet in order to use the site.

In addition to helping to drive traffic to your Ebay store, Instagram is also great for connecting with customers on a personal level by sharing photos that may not always relate directly to your business. However, as with anything you share on your business accounts, be sure to keep Instagram pictures non-controversial and lighthearted (i.e., avoid politics and religion!). Take photos of your office or of all the packages you are shipping out. Include pictures of your pets and even what you are having for lunch. Make it your goal to post at least one photo to Instagram every day.

Hashtags are a big part of getting your content on Instagram found. I like to include three to five hashtags with every photo I share. When I post a photo related to Ebay, I use hashtags such as "Ebay," "Ebayer," "Reseller," "Picker," "Thrifting," "MakingMoneyOnline," "WorkFromHome," "EbaySeller," or "self-employed." The goal of these hashtags is that people will search for them and find me.

Instagram allows you to include one website link in your profile; so, if you are using Instagram to bring in Ebay customers, you will want to make that the link to your Ebay Store. And while you can include the link when you share a photo, it won't be active. Therefore, a tip is to put something like, "25% off sale going on right now in our Ebay store; direct link in profile @yourinstagramaccount. The "@" link will take users to your profile page where the active link to your Ebay Store will be. Then the user simply clicks on your Ebay Store URL, taking them straight to your Ebay listings.

Some sellers are also using Instagram to sell items directly, skipping Ebay altogether. Many sellers will put up a picture of an item and offer it up for sale right on Instagram. All someone has to do is message the poster (Instagram has a "mailbox" system that allows users to message one another) to give them their email so the seller can send them a PayPal invoice.

Just like with Facebook, Twitter, and Pinterest, you will want to network with other Ebay sellers and even your customers by following them back on Instagram and "liking" their posts. Include the link to your Instagram page on your blog/website, package enclosures, and Facebook page. And share your Instagram link periodically on Facebook and Twitter. While I have a main "Ann Eckhart" Instagram account, I also have a second account dedicated specifically to my Ebay store.

TikTok: TikTok is the newest entry into the social media world and is promoted as a video-sharing social network. The TikTok app allows users to create short-form mobile videos. The platform has a vast catalog of sounds and song clips along with special effects and filters. Other users can "react" to TikToks, allowing them to record their reactions in side-by-side frames to other creators' content. TikTok is growing by the day as more users, particularly celebrities, join the app.

As with any fast-growing platform, businesses are jumping on the TikTok bandwagon, too; and as an Ebay seller, you can also leverage it to drive traffic to your listings. By creating a TikTok account and putting the link to your Ebay store in your profile, you can potentially attract customers by showing off newly listed items.

YouTube: A blog/website. Facebook. Twitter. Pinterest. Instagram. TikTok. Are you feeling overwhelmed? Take a deep breath and relax; no one expects you to master these social networking sites and techniques in one day. Take one at a time before moving on to the next one. Once you've mastered the second site, continue on to the third, and so on.

We've already covered the biggest sites Ebay sellers are using to drive sales and make more money, but there are still others you can use, including YouTube. Not only can you use YouTube to drive traffic to your Ebay listings, but you can also make money on your videos through Google's AdSense program.

But what kind of videos can you make that will help you increase your Ebay sales? One way to use YouTube to help sell your Ebay items is to take videos of products you have listed and include those videos in your Ebay listings. And you can also share the video via your other social media accounts, hoping that viewers will click through to the actual listing.

Note that making videos can be time-consuming, so shooting a video for every single item you have listed would likely not be worth it, especially for lower priced items. However, for items you are selling that have moving parts, play music, or are higher priced, adding a video to the listing may help sell it.

Under every YouTube video is a description box where you can include information as well as links. I include the links to my *Amazon Author Page,* blog, and all social media accounts under my videos so that viewers can easily click on the links to visit my various sites.

What many Ebay sellers do to grow their sales via YouTube is to make videos showing new inventory they will be listing. I do haul videos on my YouTube channel showing all of the items I picked up at estate sales and thrift stores that I'll be selling on Ebay. Not only does this help educate others about how they can make money on Ebay, but it also lets customers know what items will be showing up in my Ebay store soon.

However, more than driving sales, making videos about your

Ebay business is really about connecting with other sellers. Selling on Ebay can be a bit lonely when you don't know anyone else who does it. And chances are your friends and family don't understand what you do (or they just want you to sell their stuff for them). By sharing your Ebay business through YouTube videos and by searching out others, you'll quickly find yourself networking will fellow resellers. And once you connect on YouTube, you can also connect on Facebook, Twitter, and other social networks.

You may think Ebay sellers compete with one another, but I've found the opposite to be true. People who sell on Ebay love meeting others who do, too. They enjoy watching YouTube videos about selling on Ebay, and they support each other on social networking.

And if you, like me, source secondhand items to resell on Ebay (from thrift stores, garage sales, and estate sales), YouTube is a fantastic resource to learn what items to look for to make money. When I transitioned from selling new gift items to secondhand goods, YouTube videos helped teach me what items to look for when I was out "picking."

You don't need a fancy camera or high-price editing software to make YouTube videos. I actually film mine on an iPhone! After you upload a video, you can monetize it so that it brings in AdSense revenue. And once your video goes live, you can share it to social media via the convenient "share" icons YouTube provides under each video.

I make all kinds of Ebay related videos, including the hauls I mentioned earlier. I've also filmed lots of how-to videos teaching people everything from how to list items to what shipping materials I use.

For more information about YouTube, be sure to check out my book **How to Start a YouTube Channel for Fun & Profit** (the link to my *Amazon Author Page* is at the end of this book).

LinkedIn: LinkedIn is a social networking site specifically for the business community. Rather than sharing family photos as you do on Facebook, you want to keep LinkedIn strictly professional by only sharing your business content such as blog posts and Tweets related to your Ebay business.

Creating a LinkedIn account is free and easy, and you can automatically connect your account with your other social networking sites. As with Facebook, LinkedIn allows you to connect with fellow users. You can search out friends and past co-workers. Think of LinkedIn as an online resume where you highlight your past accomplishments and share your current business activities.

I have my LinkedIn account set up so that my blog posts are automatically shared there. Those who I have connected with on LinkedIn can then click through to my blog if interested, and from there, they can find my Ebay listings.

Does my LinkedIn activity bring me any Ebay customers? Not really. However, since it is free to create an account, it's something you should take the time to do to add to your social media presence. There are Ebay seller groups on LinkedIn that you may want to check out, too. And if you are open to selling on consignment, LinkedIn could be a way to find clients.

Putting It All Together: When you sell on Ebay, your first and foremost concern should be creating new Ebay listings, sourcing new inventory, answering customer questions, and shipping out orders. A good title, photos, and description are crucial to creating an Ebay listing that will result in a sale. Think of social media as the final step in that listing creation process.

As I have mentioned several times before, Ebay makes it easy to share your listings to Facebook, Twitter, and Pinterest via "share" buttons located in every active listing. After I finish creating a listing, I click on the active link and go to the upper right-hand side of the page where the "share" buttons are. I click through to each one and post my listings to the respective sites. Note that connecting your Ebay account to your social media networks is a one-time step; once you have set up the connections, they will remain linked. It only takes about 15 seconds for me to share a listing out to the three main social media sites, a little longer if I add in hashtags.

One tip is that if you are listing a large batch of items, share each individually to Twitter and Pinterest but hold off on Facebook. Why? I talked before about how Facebook likes to "hide" business page posts, only showing your page followers a limited number of posts. So, if you flood Facebook with link after link, Facebook will hide most of them from your followers' feeds. Instead, wait until you have finished listing for the day and then post a photo of the items you listed to Facebook with a link to your Ebay store. I like to use an app for creating photo collages to make one photo showing several items. Facebook tends to show individual photos over direct links, so it's much more likely followers will actually see the one photo you and click through to your listings through it.

If you are using Instagram, try posting a photo at least a few times a week. You can upload shots of your office, new inventory, or even what you are having for lunch. Include three to five hashtags so that users can find you. And be sure you are following other users and "liking" their content, too. I like to spend a few minutes scrolling through my Instagram feed to connect with other users at the end of the day.

Having a blog/website and/or YouTube channel will add a considerable amount of more work for you, so only use them if you feel they are benefitting your sales or you are getting something from them personally (as in networking with other sellers). If you do utilize those options, be sure to share the content you create over to all of your other social networking sites.

When I upload a new YouTube video, I share it with Facebook, Twitter, and Pinterest using the "share" buttons under the video; and I also post it to my blog. Again, that post then gets sent to readers who have signed up for the blog post alerts.

While I put in a lot of effort to market my Ebay Store online, I also have promotional tools I use offline. As I mentioned earlier, I include a packing slip in all of my Ebay orders (you can print these directly from PayPal after your shipping label has printed); and I also include a business card sized "thank you" note in all packages (I order these from VistaPrint). The cards contain my Ebay store URL in the hope customers will come back to shop with me. It also gives orders a personal touch that helps cultivate positive feedback.

EBAY MARKETING TOOLS: While the various social media sites help advertise your Ebay business, you can also utilize several features directly through Ebay to drive sales.

In the **Seller Hub**, click on the **Marketing tab** at the top of the page. Here you will be able to access:

- **Branding for your Ebay store**
- **Promotions**
- **Markdown sale**
- **Advertising via Promoted Listings**

Clicking on the **Store** link will take you to a page where you can edit your Ebay store information, including your:

- **Store name** (you can change your store name at any time)
- **Billboard** (an image that expresses your brand, shows your products, or announces a promotion or event; also referred to as a "banner"))
- **Logo** (300px x 300pm and 12MB max file size)
- **Description** (a short blub about you and what you sell; it will appear when buyers search for your store on Ebay)
- **Featured Listings** (great if you sell multi-quantity items, although you can opt not to show any Featured Listings)

- **Listings** (select the order in which you want items displayed in your store as well as the layout)
- **Category Type** (choose either Ebay OR your own store categories to display on the left navigation bar of your store)

Promotions: Under **MERCHANDISING** on the left-hand column in the *Marketing* section of your *Seller Hub* is the **Promotions** link. Ebay has recently added a lot of new ways for us to promote our listings, including:

- **Order size discounts** that incentivize buyers to spend more money in your store by setting minimum discounts, such as B1G1 FREE offers and percentage/dollar off discounts on quantity and order total minimums.
- **Shipping discounts** that let buyers save on shipping when they buy more from you.
- **Codeless coupons** that allow you to create URL's that you can share via social media and email that give your customers percentage or dollar-off discounts.
- **Volume pricing** incentivizes buyers to buy more quantities of your items by setting discounts on multi-quantity purchases such as "save 15% when you buy two or more items".

Markdown Sale: Back over on the left-hand side of the *Marketing* page is the **Markdown sale** link. This is the feature I use the most when trying to drive sales; Ebay used to call it **Markdown Manager**. By clicking on the **blue Create a promotion button** on the upper right-hand side of the page and choosing **Sale event + markdown** from the drop-down menu, you will be taken to the **Create a sale event** page.

Ebay offers you three different Choose your discount options:

- **Take a percent off each item** (the drop-down menu offers you the option of anywhere from 5% to 80% off)
- **Take a dollar amount off of each item** (the drop-down

menu offers you the option of anywhere from $5 to $1500 off)
- **Free shipping for all discounted items** (in addition to the percentage or dollar amount discount)

Let's say you want to run a 30% off sale. You would enter "30" as the percentage off discount and then click on the **blue Select items button.** You will then be taken to a new screen where you can **Select Items individually** OR **Create rules using categories.** I have always used the *Select Items individually* option, but you can play around with both choices to see which you like best.

When I choose to *Select Items individually*, I am taken to a new screen where I can see all of my active *Fixed Price* listings. I can select all of my items or narrow them down by **category, price**, and/or **days on site**. I can bulk select everything I have listed or manually check each item I want to be placed into the sale. I typically run my sales on all of the items in my store, so I usually just auto select all of my listings. Note that you can only select up to 500 listings for each sale you create, so if you have a large store, the *Create rules using categories* option may work better for you. There's no way that's better than the other; it just depends on what works best for you.

Back to the sale example: You've chosen to *Select Items* individually. Let's say that you have 400 items listed; you can easily select all of them at once to be included in your sale. You then click on the **blue Confirm selections button**, which will take you to a screen showing all of the items selected for your sale. You have the option to **Remove** any listings you want OR to click on the **blue Add more items button** before clicking on the **blue Save and review button.**

After clicking the **Save and review** button, the final screen to set up your sale will appear, the **Review your sale event** page. Here you can enter a Sale event name, which only you will see. You could enter "30% off sale", for instance. You'll be able to **review your Discount type and items** (in this case, 30% off 400 items;

you have another chance here to edit these options).

Next is the **Date range**. You will need to select a start date and time AND an end date and time. I typically set my sale to start immediately and to end a week later. Finally, under the **Sale event banner**, you type in your **Sale event description** ("Save 30% Off Everything!" as an example) and **Select sale event image** (Ebay will give you three of your listing thumbnails to choose from, or you can upload a different one).

The last section of this page is the **Preview sale event tile,** which shows you what customers will see on their end. If everything looks good, you simply click on the **blue Launch button** at the bottom of the page to start your sale!

Note that you can pause, edit, or end your sale at any time. It can take Ebay an hour or two to get your sale up and running, so don't worry if you don't see your items marked down immediately after you click on *Launch*. Once your sale is live, be sure to promote it via social media and on your website, if you have one.

Promoted Listings: You can utilize the free social media platforms to drive customers to your Ebay store. And Ebay allows you to run sales for free, too. However, you will want to consider one more piece of marketing, although it is not free; and that is *Promoted Listings.*

Promoted Listings are a relatively new offering from Ebay, and it's is one that I myself use all day, every day. With so many other people selling on Ebay, I've found that I need to pay for *Promoted Listings* in order to remain competitive.

Ebay describes *Promoted Listings* as helping "your items stand out among billions of listings on Ebay and be seen by millions of active buyers when they're browsing and searching for what you are selling, helping to increase the likelihood of a sale. You only pay when an item sells. *Promoted Listings* is available only to Above Standard and Top-Rated Sellers with recent sales activity".

Ebay points to four key benefits of *Promoted Listings:*

1. **Boost Visibility:** Your items are more likely to sell when more people see them. *Promoted Listings* puts your items in front of more buyers, boosting visibility by up to 36%.
2. **Pay Only For Sale:** You're not charged until a buyer clicks on your promoted listing and purchases the promoted item within 30 days.
3. **Guided Set-Up:** Ebay's guidance tools help take the guesswork out and suggest which items to promote and at what cost.
4. **Detailed Reporting:** Access detailed campaign metrics and sales reports to monitor performance and fine-tune your campaigns.

From **Seller Hub,** click on **Marketing** and choose **Promoted listings** from the drop-down menu. Here you will see the **Summary** date of any *Promoted listings* you have already run, and you can set up a new campaign by clicking on the **blue Create new campaign button** near the bottom of the page.

After clicking on *Create new campaign*, a new screen will appear titled **How do you want to create your campaign?** You have two choices: **Select listings individually** OR **Select listings in bulk**. I always choose the *Select listings individually* option as, for me, it is actually easier than the bulk option.

By choosing to *Select listings individually*, a new screen comes up where I can select each eligible item to add to my *Promoted Listing.* When I run *Promoted Listing* campaigns, I include all of the items in my store, making a simple bulk selection to choose all of my listings. I then click on the **blue Set ad rate button** to continue to the Set ad rates screen. Ebay offers a walk-through tutorial on this page if you would like more guidance. Note that your ad rate is the percentage of the final sale price, excluding shipping and taxes, that you are willing to pay to have your listing promoted.

You cannot set ad rates below 1% or above 100%. You are only charged a fee when your item sells within 30 days of the customer clicking on it.

Ebay will default to showing you their **Suggested ad rates,** which are typically relatively high. My trick is to click on the **blue Change your ad rate strategy button** and select **Apply single ad rate.** I then choose a rate of 1% or 2% for all of my items. I have found this to be just as successful as choosing the Ebay suggested rates, but it saves me a lot of money as I'm not paying the higher percentage.

After choosing my rate, I click on the **blue Review button** at the bottom of the page. The third and final screen is brought up, which is **Name your campaign.** I enter a name that only I will see (Ebay makes you write something in this field, but buyers won't see it). I then click on the **blue Launch button** at the bottom of the screen to start the *Promoted Listings* campaign.

After click on the *Launch* button, you'll be taken back to the main *Promoted listings* page that you started at. At the bottom of this page, you will see your **Campaigns,** both active and ended. Ebay will default to running your campaigns continuously, but I personally like to have my campaigns run for shorter periods, anywhere from a week to a month. I've found them to be more successful when they have an end date, and I then start a brand-new campaign. And just as with running a sale, you can pause, edit, or end your *Promoted Listings* at any time.

A website, social media papers, branding, sales, and promoting listings are so many options available to you as an Ebay seller. While it can all seem overwhelming, trust me that promotion efforts become second nature after a while. The increase in sales will make all of your extra time and effort worth it in the end!

CHAPTER FOUR: HOW TO MANAGE YOUR EBAY STORE

To open an Ebay store or not? That is the question I have been asked more times than I can count since I started giving out Ebay advice in my books and on my YouTube channel!

The general rule of thumb is that if you consistently have at least 100 items listed on Ebay, then an Ebay store makes sense financially. Ebay store owners get discounts on both listing and final value fees. Ebay currently offers five different store subscriptions:

Starter Store:

- $4.95 a month when you commit to an annual subscription
- 250 free fixed-price listings per month
- 30-cent fixed price listing fee above allocation
- 10% final value fee in most categories

Basic Store:

- $21.95 a month when you commit to an annual subscription

- 350 free fixed-price listings per month
- 250 free auction listings for collectibles and fashion
- 25-cent fixed-price listing fee above allocation
- 25-cent auction listing fee above allocation
- $25 Ebay branded shipping supply coupon every quarter
- 4-9.15% final value fee on most items
- Free subscription to *Terapeak Research* tool

Premium Store:

- $59.95 a month for 1,000 fixed-price listings
- 1,000 free fixed-price listings per month
- 500 free auction listings for collectibles and fashion
- 10-cent fixed-price listing fee above allocation
- 15-cent auction listing fee above allocation
- $50 Ebay branded shipping supply coupon every quarter
- 4-9.15% final value fee on most items
- Free subscription to *Terapeak Research* tool

Anchor Store:

- $299.95 a month for 10,000 fixed-price listings
- 10,000 free fixed-price listings per month
- 1,000 free auction listings for collectibles and fashion
- 5-cent fixed-price listing fee above allocation
- 10-cent auction listing fee above allocation
- $150 Ebay branded shipping supply coupon every quarter
- $25 towards Promoted Listings every quarter
- 4-9.15% final value fee on most items
- Free subscription to *Terapeak Research* tool
- Access to dedicated customer support by phone or email

Enterprise:

- $2,999.95 a month for 100,000 fixed-price listings
- 100,000 free fixed-price listings per month
- 2,500 free auction listings for collectibles and fashion
- 5-cent fixed-price listing fee above allocation
- 10-cent auction listing fee above allocation
- $150 Ebay branded shipping supply coupon every quarter
- $25 towards Promoted Listings every quarter
- 4-9.15% final value fee on most items
- Free subscription to *Terapeak Research* tool
- Access to dedicated customer support by phone or email
- Access to free sales-tax calculation assistance from Vertex

All Ebay Store subscribers receive:

- Access to Promoted Listings
- Access to Promotions Manager
- Customizable Storefront Homepage
- Customized Store Web Address
- Controllable "Featured Items"
- Store Categories

My favorite features of having an Ebay store are:

A personalized URL (web address) that you can give customers to send them directly to your store. This shorted URL is easy to put on business cards or other enclosures. I include my URL store link on all of my social media sites, in my books, and on YouTube to drive traffic directly to my store.

The ability to personalize your Ebay store's look by changing the colors, adding your logo, and utilizing "Pages" to provide your customers with more information. To access these customization tools, go to your Ebay store's front page and click on the **Manage My Store** button in the upper right-hand corner of the page. There are a lot of features here to explore under the **Store**

Management column on the left-hand side of the page, including:

Advertising Preferences: Ebay allows you to control the information you share regarding how the site uses cookies, partners with advertisers, and collects information from your devices. You can edit these selections, i.e., turn them off or on at any time. Mine is always set to "No."

Permissions: Add authorized users, such as employees, to your Ebay account

Store Categories: One of the best of having an Ebay store is the ability to create specific item categories. Not only can buyers narrow down their search when they are looking at your store, but it is helpful for you as a seller to keep track of your inventory.

The great thing about categories is you can add and delete them as you see fit. Perhaps you have a large stock of camera equipment to sell, so you create a "Camera" category. However, after you have sold all of the cameras, you can delete the "Camera" category or simply leave it in your store set up as only categories with active listings show up. Inactive categories will still be visible to you in the "Manage Your Store" section, but they will only be seen by customers if or when you add items to them.

I like to arrange my categories alphabetically. While you can break down categories into subcategories, you are usually fine merely listing in the main category unless you have thousands of items listed.

Make sure to spell and capitalize your categories appropriately. I like to put mine in all capitals, such as "COLLECTIBLES" and "COFFEE MUGS." I personally think typing a category like "BIBLES & HYMNALS" looks a lot better than "bibles and hymnals." However, if I add in sub-categories, I type them in sentence case, i.e., "Bibles and Hymnals."

Once you have an Ebay store, you will be able to select the store categories for your items whenever you go to list something. You can list in two store categories. Note that the store categories are different from the Ebay categories, where you get one free and have to pay for a second. With your store categories, both selections are free.

Edit Store: *Customize your Store Name, Billboard (banner), Log, Description, Featured Listings,* and *Display*

Subscriber Discounts: Here is where you can access your **quarterly Ebay Shipping Supply Coupon** (for *Starter, Premium, Anchor,* and *Enterprise* store levels). Every quarter, Ebay provides a shipping supply coupon that you can apply towards Ebay branded shipping supplies, including boxes, poly and bubble mailers, shipping tape, tissue paper, and stickers. TIP: Always spend a little bit more than your shipping coupon amount. You can only use your coupon code ONCE, so if you don't spend it all the first time, you will lose any overage. My favorite shipping supplies are the stickers!

Other discounts for store subscribers include Gusto Payroll, Bench Bookkeeping, Ebay Wholesale Deals, PayPal Shopping Offers, and Frootion Design Services.

Email Marketing: A rarely discussed feature of having an Ebay Store is that you can promote it by sending emails to anyone who adds you to their *Saved Sellers List.* You can also offer a *Store newsletter link* on your store's homepage. Ebay provides you with several user-friendly templates for you to customize when you want to update your subscribers about any sales, special promotions, or exciting new items in your store.

Listing Frame: Set up a custom listing frame that will appear in all of your listings. It can include your store's listing header and a left-navigation bar with links to your store's categories. This is a fun section to play around with in order to give your listings a customized look

Note that some links are repeated under the *Manage Your Store* page, such as *Permissions* and *Advertisement Preferences.* Also,

Manage Promotions and *Markdown Manager* will take you back over to those sections of your *Seller Hub* that we discussed earlier in this chapter. The *Manage Your Store* page has gone through some changes in recent years, especially now that *Seller Hub,* not **My Ebay**, is the main page Ebay sellers use to manage their accounts.

Time Away: While only Ebay Store subscribers used to be able to put their stores and listings on vacation, now all Ebay users have access to what is now referred to as **Time Away**. Whether you need a break due to personal reasons or you are going on a vacation, anyone who sells on Ebay can now **Schedule Time Away.** You can choose to allow sales to continue by editing your handling time, or you can pause your sales until you return. I always choose to pause sales as if I'm unable to have my store open; it is because I am too busy to attend to it properly. Therefore, I don't want to have to deal with customer questions. By pausing sales, your items are still visible on Ebay's site, but buyers cannot purchase them. *The Time Away* feature only applies to *Fixed Price* items, so make sure you have ended all *Auctions* before activating the *Time Away* feature.

If my Ebay sales are slow, I use the trick of turning my *Time Away* settings on overnight and then back off the next day. This seems to cause my listings to get "rebooted" in the Ebay system and showing up as newly listed items. While there is no official word from Ebay that this is true, most sellers report that they see a spike in sales after using the *Time Away* feature. I have always gotten sales when I reactivated my listings the following day. I refer to this as "jiggling my store switch"!

To access your *Time Away* options, click on the **My Ebay** link at the top of your Ebay account page. Click on the **Account tab,** and you'll find **Time Away** linked under **Selling** on the left-hand column of the page.

Store vs. No Store: One of the most common questions I get about selling on Ebay is whether or not to open a store. As I mentioned earlier, the general rule of thumb is that if you are consistently going to have at least 100 items listed on Ebay, then a store makes the most financial sense. If you haven't already subscribed to an Ebay store, you can always start with the lowest level and upgrade later. If you sign up for a store under the yearly rate, not the month-to-month rate, note that if you cancel or downgrade your store before your year is up that you will have to pay the difference from the monthly and yearly rate.

Sellers often feel that they have to get their Ebay store "ready" before opening it to the public. However, you need to remember that an Ebay store isn't like a brick-and-mortar store. The vast majority of customers will access your listings in Ebay's search, not through your actual store. It will only be after you start promoting your store's URL address via social media that people will actually get to your storefront to see what you have for sale. Once you subscribe to an Ebay store, your listings will automatically be placed there. You can't hide your store from users until you deem it "ready."

While I encourage you to have a great store design, your first priority should be getting your items listed. Once a listing is live, it will automatically be visible in your Ebay store. If you find that your sales are going well and that your listings are increasing, you can always upgrade your store subscription level; in fact, Ebay will likely message you with special offers to upgrade your store if it is performing well.

Many sellers think having an Ebay Store is all about the customer's experience. But the truth is that sellers gain a lot more from a store in terms of reduced fees and organization than buyers do from shopping in a "store" setting. Because most customers will find your listings in Ebay's search, many will not click through your actual Ebay Store. But even though most buyers won't venture into your "store," it doesn't mean you shouldn't have one as the savings on listing fees alone is typically worth the price of your subscription!

CHAPTER FIVE: BEST BUSINESS PRACTICES

Even if you follow all of the tips and tricks in this book designed to avoid most customer problems, you will inevitably occasionally run into issues when selling on Ebay. Fortunately, Ebay provides several safeguards to protect both buyers and sellers. You want to resolve all issues through Ebay's messaging and reporting systems; do not attempt to problem solve through direct email or by phone. Doing so will void any seller's protection you may be eligible for.

In business, the customer is always right (even when you know they are actually wrong!), so it's essential to have a good set of customer policies in place so that both you and the buyer understand what is expected of one another. Ebay, of course, has its own set of policies that you must adhere to, such as giving buyers two business days to pay for their items. You can't demand someone pay you within an hour as that is not Ebay's rule. When you sell on Ebay, you must first follow Ebay's rules. Ebay isn't YOUR business; it is a TOOL you use in your business.

As I talked about earlier, there is no better way to learn about listing on Ebay than to note what other sellers are doing by buying a few things yourself, reading books, and watching "how-to" videos on YouTube. And while I have already shared some of the following tips with you, I want to reiterate some here as they are so very important to avoid issues with customers:

Accuracy: Make sure your listing titles, item specifics, and descriptions are all accurate. Any mistakes in these areas can lead to a customer filing an **Item Not As Described** (i.e., INAD) case against you.

Shipping: Charge fair shipping prices. While it is okay to slightly paid flat rate shipping costs to cover handling fees, keep your postal charges as close to the actual price as possible to avoid customers giving you a low rating on your shipping, i.e., "dinging your stars." For items weighing over a pound, I advocate using *Calculated Shipping* so that buyers pay the exact shipping cost based on the weight of the item and the zip code it is going to. Ship your items the following business day (i.e., weekday). If you get a sale on a Saturday, go ahead and print the label out and prepare it for shipment Monday. Ship your items in clean packing materials. Upgrade shipping from economy (slow) to expedited (fast) when possible to exceed your buyer's expectations.

Under-Promise & Over-Deliver: One of the best pieces of advice I got when I started selling on Ebay was to "under-promise and over-deliver." If you say you will ship items in two days, ship them in one. Print the label out as soon as you can after payment clears so that the buyer will get a notification that the item has shipped. If an item is in excellent condition, list it as "very good" so that the buyer gets more than they were expecting. Use clean packing materials and wrap items well inside of their boxes to protect them during the shipping process. Upgrade shipping when possible so that customers get their orders fast than they expect.

Returns: Ebay heavily pressures sellers not only to accept returns but to offer "free" returns, meaning the seller pays for the postage to have an item returned to them. I stopped accepting returns in 2019 as I just couldn't justify the costs. However, if you do decide to accept returns, note that Ebay's policy gives buyers 30 days to initiate a return. However, you do not have to offer "free" returns; most small sellers require that buyers pay the return shipping cost. Whatever you decide to do about returns, be sure to clearly state your policy in your description and in the "Returns" policy field within each listing.

Keeping a Schedule: To sell on Ebay successfully takes a lot of WORK. Between sourcing items and listing them to answering customer questions and preparing shipments, it is easy for Ebay to take up every waking moment of your life. While attending to customers and shipping out items should always take priority, it is also important to set realistic goals for each day so that you don't get overwhelmed.

What has worked for me is to go out "picking" (i.e., shopping at estate sales and thrift stores, often referred to these days as "sourcing") only on certain days. I take photos and only take photos on another day. On the days that I am not sourcing or taking pictures, I list. By only focusing on one area of business on a given day, I am able to commit to it fully and not get overwhelmed by trying to do it all in a single day. The only tasks I do every single day are answering customer questions and shipping out orders.

I also make sure to take some time off now and then. A day or two off from Ebay ensures that you don't burn out on your business. Even a few hours away from the computer to do something fun like meeting a friend for lunch or going window shopping can help you come back to Ebay with renewed energy. After all, you likely started a home-based business so that you would have more freedom and time with your family, so don't forget to take time for yourself!

Filing an Unpaid Bidder Claim: Nothing is more frustrating than selling an item on Ebay only to have the buyer not pay. Fortunately, you can take steps to either get the customer to initiate their payment or to recoup your fees and relist the item.

First of all, it's important to remember that Ebay gives buyers two days to pay. Therefore, you can't demand payment within an hour of a sale. While you can change your *Fixed Price* listings to require *Immediate Payment,* this option does not work for *Auctions.* There is no point in telling auction winners that they have to pay immediately as those are not Ebay's rules. Remember, Ebay is a TOOL you are using in your business. Ebay is NOT your business, so you have to follow THEIR rules.

After an *Auction* ends, Ebay will notify the winner that they need to make payment. However, if they don't pay within an hour, I will then send the buyer an invoice. This is easy to do as it is an option in the drop-down menu next to the item in your *Orders* section of *Seller Hub.* Usually, the buyer will pay by the end of the day. However, if by the next day I still haven't received payment, I will send the buyer a reminder to pay. Ebay makes this easy to do as they have a "reminder" feature you can click on to send a pre-filled message to the customer.

If you are confused about what day the buyer has until to pay, simply choose "Resolve a Problem" from the drop-down menu next to the item in "My Ebay." By then selecting the "I haven't received my payment" option, Ebay will tell you when you can file a claim.

If I still haven't received payment by the third day after sending an invoice and a reminder, I will then open a claim. Ebay then contacts the buyer themselves to let them know that they need to make payment immediately, or they will get an unpaid item strike. The vast majority of the time, this is enough to get the buyer to pay. However, buyers have four days from Ebay's warning to make payment. If you haven't gotten your money after that additional four days, you can close the claim case and recoup all of your listing and final value fees.

If a buyer ends up not paying and I have to file a claim and then close a case, I then relist the item and block the buyer. I simply highlight and copy the buyer's Ebay screen and go to the **Blocked Buyers List** on Ebay's site. Ebay doesn't make finding this page easy, so I recommend that you do a simple internet search for

"Ebay blocked bidders list" to find this page, and then bookmark it for future reference.

During this entire process, the only direct contact I make with the buyer is the ONE message reminding them that their payment is due. I don't message them several times a day. I don't message them telling them I'm filing a claim. And I don't message them that they've been blocked. I let Ebay handle all communication with the buyer, which they will do by sending them a message about the unpaid claim and warning them that they will get a strike if they don't submit payment.

Reporting Buyers: I always say that 99.9% of my Ebay customers are fantastic and that only .01% ever cause me problems. However, when someone is being mean or threatening online, it often feels like everyone is against you.

Fortunately, if someone is harassing you, you can report them to Ebay. Ebay is not only proactive when it comes to getting bad sellers off of the site, but in recent years, they have begun to crack down harder on bad buyers, too.

Suppose someone has sent you an inappropriate message through the Ebay messaging system (trying to extort feedback or cussing at you). In that case, you can easily report them through the link provided in the **Marketplace Safety Tip** box under the message. Simply click on the **Report an inappropriate email** link. Ebay will then be able to see the message for themselves and take action.

Don't engage with a threatening buyer yourself; simply ignore them and report them to Ebay. I also take the step to block them so that they can't buy anything else from me. Again, by keeping all communication on Ebay's site, Ebay has a record of any threats or harassment, and they can take action on their end, which prevents you from having to further deal with problem customers.

Ebay Support: Ebay support is available by phone or through messaging, although they do not make it easy to get in touch with a service representative. First, you will need to go to your **Seller**

Hub and click on the **Seller Help** link in the page's upper right-hand corner. Here you can contact Ebay regarding the following issues:

- Request to remove improper feedback
- Request to remove defects that you believe to be out of your control
- Request a selling limit increase, which they will often grant if you've been meeting your seller performance standards
- Report an issue with a buyer who is not following Ebay's policies

If none of the above options apply to your situation, you can click on the **Need more help?** link at the bottom of the page. This will take you to Ebay's **Customer Service Selling** page with links to articles explaining all of Ebay's policies. However, if you scroll all the way to the bottom of the page, there is another **Need more help?** section with a link for **Contact us.**

Once again, you will be brought to a page with various articles related to the problem you have identified. And again, at the bottom of this page is the third **Need more help?** area, although now you can choose to **Chat with our automated system** OR **Have us call you**. The call option will show you the wait time you can expect to receive a call.

Privacy/Safety: While the internet offers a level of anonymity, when you are on Ebay, there are some extra precautions you want to take. First and foremost is guarding your Ebay account information. Change your passwords often, and make them a combination of letters, numbers, and characters so that they will be nearly impossible to hack. The same goes for your PayPal account if you still aren't enrolled in *Managed Payments.*

The only legitimate messages from Ebay will come to you via the Ebay messaging system that you access when you are logged into your account. At the tops of your **Seller Hub** page is a link for **Messages**. Unless you have opted for copies of all messages that Ebay sends to you also be emailed to you, then the official messages from Ebay will only be found here. Ebay does not send sellers direct email messages off of the site; so, if you get an email from Ebay that isn't also found in your *Messages* box, know that it is a scam. Scammers have been known to send emails to sellers disguised as messages from Ebay saying that you need to click a link within the email to reset your password or to login into your account. NEVER click on these email links, and do not give your Ebay or PayPal information to anyone claiming to be from the companies either by phone or email. Again, only use the *Messages* system through your Ebay account. And when in doubt, contact Ebay directly using the steps I laid out in the previous section of this chapter.

Keeping your home address private is another concern for Ebay sellers. I myself never worried too much about this until recently, when I finally got a P.O. Box so that I could make that my return mailing address for packages. Remember that your address will print out with your shipping label, so if you send out a lot of packages, you may want to make that address someplace other than home (such as your spouses' work or a P.O. Box). While this shouldn't be a huge concern (after all, people have been using their home addresses for years), it may be something you want to consider.

I have a designated email set up expressly for Ebay in which all Ebay and PayPal communications go to. Although some large sellers, typically those with warehouses or brick-and-mortar stores, do set up a number specifically for Ebay customers to call, I personally guard my phone number.

I also do not engage with customers outside of the Ebay system. Several times over the years, buyers have gotten a hold of my phone number and called my house, leaving me messages asking me to return their calls. I do not return calls from anyone who calls my home, nor should you. I do the same with direct emails;

I delete them without responding. If an Ebay customer wants to communicate with me, they need to contact me directly through Ebay's *Messages* system.

Ebay Selling Practices Policy: It is important to remember that you need to adhere to Ebay's rules in order to utilize their site. As I have said before, Ebay is not YOUR business; it is a TOOL you use for your business. Ebay has given us the following policies, which all sellers are expected to follow:

- Promptly resolve customer issues
- Ship items on time, within your specified handling time
- Manage inventory and keep items well stocked
- Charge reasonable shipping and handling costs
- Specify shipping costs and handling time in the listing
- Follow through on your return policy
- Respond to buyers' questions promptly
- Be helpful, friendly, and professional throughout a transaction.
- Make sure the item is delivered to the buyer as described in the listing

Ebay warns sellers that not meeting buyers' expectations can result in the following issues for sellers:

- Not meeting the late shipment rate requirements
- Exceeding minimum requirements for the defect rate
- A bad experience for you and the buyer
- Low detailed seller ratings
- Negative or neutral feedback from a buyer
- A buyer requesting a return or reporting that an item was not received

- A buyer asking us to step in and help with a transaction issue

And issues with buyers affect your **Ebay's Transaction Defect Rate Requirements,** which is the percentage of transactions that have one or both of the following defects:

- eBay Money Back Guarantee and PayPal Purchase Protection cases closed without seller resolution
- Seller-initiated transaction cancellation

To meet Ebay's minimum standard selling requirements, sellers can only have up to 2% of transactions with one or more defects over the most recent evaluation period. To qualify as a **Top-Rated Seller**, which not only places your listings higher in search but also gives you fee discounts, you can only have up to 0.5% of transactions with one or more defects over the most recent evaluation period. Note that only your transactions with US buyers count towards your seller performance rating.

According to Ebay, "The defect rate won't affect your seller performance status until you have transactions with defects with at least five different buyers, or at least four different buyers to impact Top-Rated status within your evaluation period. You can have a maximum of 0.3% of eBay Money Back Guarantee or PayPal Purchase Protection closed cases without seller resolution over the most recent evaluation period. That means the buyer reported they didn't receive an item, asked to return an item, or opened a PayPal Purchase Protection case, you weren't able to resolve it, the buyer asked us to step in and help, and we found you responsible."

"Sellers with 400 or more transactions over the past three months are evaluated based on the past three months, and sellers with fewer than 400 transactions are evaluated based on the past 12 months. Buyers won't see your defect rate. Keep in mind that buyers still see your feedback rating and all four detailed seller ratings."

In regards to shipping defects, Ebay states that sellers will "be recognized for on-time shipping if tracking shows your item was either shipped within the stated handling time or delivered by the estimated delivery date. If there's no tracking available, we'll check with your buyer. If your buyer confirms the item was delivered on time—you'll be recognized for on-time shipping."

Ebay will only consider a shipment as late if:

- Tracking shows the item was delivered after the estimated delivery date **unless** there's an acceptance scan within your handling time or there's confirmation from the buyer of on-time delivery.
- The buyer confirms the item was delivered after the estimated delivery date **unless** there's an acceptance scan within your handling time or there's delivery confirmation by the estimated delivery date.

Ebay's Money Back Guarantee: Buyer can have confidence when shopping on Ebay due to the site's *Money Back Guarantee.* And while this policy can frustrate sellers who may feel that a buyer is taking advantage of them, the policy is in place to ensure that all customers feel safe when shopping on Ebay so that they will return to the site again and again.

According to Ebay, "When a buyer initially starts a return because the item didn't match the listing description or reports that they didn't receive an item, the transaction issue is called a "request." If the buyer and seller can't resolve the problem, and the buyer or seller asks us to step in and help with the transaction, the request then becomes a "case."

"For **PayPal Purchase Protection**, the transaction issue is a "case" throughout the process. The number of cases closed without resolution is an essential indicator of how well a seller may be meeting buyer expectations on eBay and is a measure of overall seller performance. A case closed without seller resolution is any case the seller is unable to resolve with the buyer before the buyer asking us to step in and help with a request, or escalating a case to PayPal for review, and eBay or PayPal determines the seller is responsible."

These policies are not just public relations soundbites; they are what Ebay uses to evaluate our seller performance standards, which allow us to continue selling on their site. However, Ebay also offers many **Seller Protections,** including their **Abusive Buyer Policy**, which prohibits buyers from:

- Demanding something that wasn't offered in the original listing
- Making false claims about an order
- Misusing returns
- Misusing Ebay's messaging system or bidding platform
- Abusing the buyer protection program

Ebay also recognizes that some situations are out of both the seller's and buyer's hands; fortunately, they offer protections for events outside of a seller's control, including:

If an item arrives late, but tracking shows that you shipped it on time, Ebay will automatically adjust your late shipment rate and remove feedback as long as the carrier scan show you shipped within your handling time; or the carrier scan shows that the item arrived by the estimated delivery, even if you shipped it late

If there is no tracking, the order won't be counted as late as long as the buyer doesn't indicate that it was late. This could happen if perhaps you mailed a small, flat item via *First Class Letter* mail, or your postal carrier didn't scan the shipment. Ebay is also particularly good about protecting sellers due to severe weather or other carrier disruptions by automatically adjusting the late shipment rate, removing canceled transaction defects, and removing feedback as long as you are in an area identified as experiencing delivery delays, as long as the shipment receives a carrier scan within you handling time. However, it is still late due to weather, or Ebay instructs you to hold a shipment or cancel a transaction altogether. Ebay updates us on their **Announcement Board** as well as on the **Ebay for Business Facebook** whenever they identify a wide-spread carrier delay issue.

So, what's the best way to keep your account in good standing, even when dealing with unexpected emergencies or demanding customers? Here are my tips:

1. Make sure your listings are accurate with the correct measurements, condition, and item specifics. Also, provide lots of clear photos showing the item from every angle so that customers know exactly what they are buying.
2. Don't steal other seller's photos or use stock photos unless you have permission from the company.
3. Make sure you meet your handling time. My handling time is two business days, but I almost always ship the next business day. However, the extra day acts as a buffer in case something comes up.
4. Upgrade shipping when possible. Be sure to check all of the shipping options available when you go to print your postage. You may find that you can provide an expedited shipping service for the same cost as the economy option.
5. Respond to customer questions promptly and profes-

sionally.

6.   Package your items well to prevent breakage.

7.   If you get a return request or a message from a buyer saying the item arrived damaged, take a deep breath and direct them on how to use Ebay's return system to file a claim. Don't get into a fight via the messaging; Ebay's system is set up to handle claims and returns.

8.   If Ebay sides in a buyer's favor, it is okay to be upset but don't let it ruin your day or your business. See if there was anything you could have done differently to affect the outcome and implement those lessons as you continue selling.

9.   Do not use the Ebay messaging system for anything other than talking to Ebay customers about specific listings. Do not offer to sell something off of the Ebay site. Do not give buyers your phone number or email address. Do not reply to harassing messages, either; report those immediately to Ebay and let them handle it.

10. Over-promise and over-deliver!

CHAPTER SIX:
SCALING UP YOUR
EBAY BUSINESS

W hen you own your own business, there is no difference between part-time versus full-time in terms of the hours you will work. Selling on Ebay can be an all-day, everyday commitment; you need to be available to answer customer questions and to ship out orders promptly. If I am going to be away from my home for more than 24 hours, I put my Ebay store on vacation, now called Time Away.

When I talk about a part-time versus full-time Ebay business, I am talking about INCOME. I view a full-time Ebay business as one that provides the same income level as an average 40-hour-a-week job, enough to completely support one person by covering all of their living expenses. For some, however, a full-time income means making enough money to support an entire family. I myself work part-time *hours* of around 20 hours per week, but I bring in a full-time *income* that supports me completely.

Only you know the level of income you want and need, which will determine how many hours you put into Ebay. The great thing about Ebay is that if you want more money, you just need to put more time into putting up new listings. Consistently listing new items to Ebay is the fundamental key to making money on the site.

The vast majority of Ebay sellers who view reselling as their business are part-time. Many rely on a spouse's income for the majority of the household budget. They themselves may also work another part-time or even a full-time job in addition to Ebay to earn enough money to support their family. Benefits such as health insurance are also a big reason why many Ebay sellers have other income sources. While reselling on Ebay can be very profitable, it can be hard to cover all household expenses and insurance costs by only selling online, especially as sales can go up and down depending on the time of year. I sell a lot from October through March, but June and July are painfully slow.

However, don't let that discourage you from your dream of starting a full-time home-based Ebay business! With a ton of hard work and dedication, you CAN make a full-time living on Ebay. However, I believe it is best to start slowly by viewing an Ebay business first as a way to earn a little extra money, then expanding it to an actual part-time job. If you want to pursue it full-time after that, then go for it. If you follow the business advice in this chapter, you will already be prepared as your Ebay business grows.

Another reason you should take it slow – actually, that you may HAVE to take it slow - is that Ebay now puts limits on new sellers. So, if you are totally new to selling on Ebay, you will only be able to list a certain number of items, to begin with. Only as you prove to Ebay that you are a reputable seller will they loosen your restrictions. That is why it is so important to be careful to learn all of the ins and outs of selling on Ebay before relying on it for your income.

Perhaps you are a stay-at-home mom or dad looking to supplement your spouse's full-time income. Ebay can be an excellent job for you as it offers the flexibility of staying home with your children while running your own business. Plus, you retain the benefits from your spouses' job.

If you already have a job, I would advise keeping it and grow your Ebay business slowly. I would NEVER tell someone with a good-paying job and benefits to quit it to sell on Ebay! However, maybe you have found yourself without steady employment due to the tough job market. If you need a job NOW and see self-employment as your only option, there is no better home-based business, in my opinion, than Ebay!

Whether you go part-time or full-time, earn a few thousand dollars a year, or an income in the six figures, make sure you view Ebay as a BUSINESS! Even if you don't, Uncle Sam certainly will!

Oh, taxes! How they make people nervous! I get asked a lot about whether or not people should get a *Sales Tax Permit* and/or an *Employer Identification Number.* The answer is....IT DEPENDS!

Sales Tax Permit: If you plan to purchase items from wholesale companies, you will need a *Sales Tax Permit*. A Sales Tax Permit allows you to buy products at wholesale cost and not pay taxes on them. However, having a *Sales Tax Permit* means that you will need to collect and remit taxes on anything you sell to customers within your state.

Fortunately, Ebay now handles the collection and remittance of sales tax on the sellers' behalf. When a customer buys an item from you, if they live in a state that requires sales tax be charged, the customer will pay the sales tax, BUT Ebay will then automatically route that tax to the respective state. However, if you have a *Sale Tax Permit,* you will still have to file sales tax quarterly with your state. So, if you don't plan to use a *Sales Tax Permit* to purchase items at wholesale, you are better off not getting one so that you don't have to worry about taxes.

Employer Identification Number (EIN): An Employer Identification Number is for people who plan to hire employees. However, some wholesale companies do require an EIN to place an order from them. An EIN is free and easy to apply for. I have one since some of the wholesale companies I used to order from required it, and I still have it today as I figure I might as well just keep it rather than go through the hassle of canceling it.

There is no use in hiding from the IRS the fact that you are making money on Ebay. When you use PayPal or Managed Payments and have money deposited into your bank account, there is an on-line record of you MAKING money. If you sell enough during the course of the year, Ebay will send you a 1099 tax form; and they will send a copy of it to the IRS, too. So, to maximize deductions and increase your net profit, there are some things you will want to consider.

Insurance: If you plan on having a large supply of inventory, you will definitely want to carry business insurance to protect it in case of fire, theft, or other damage. You may also be liable for any-one who is injured coming to your home or business, including delivery people. I have paid upwards of $500 per year for busi-ness insurance. If you plan on storing thousands of dollars worth of merchandise in your home, you definitely want to consider in-suring it all.

If you plan to sell on Ebay for other people via consignment, you will definitely need to get insurance to cover any damage to or loss of their items. Call around to various insurance agencies and ask if they offer home-based business insurance coverage. If they do, ask for a free quote.

If you have a spouse whose health insurance plan you can join, you are luckier than me. I have been purchasing my own health insurance since 2005, and I have paid upwards of $600 per month for my premiums, co-pays, and prescription drugs. The **Afford-able Care Act** now makes health insurance coverage more ac-cessible and affordable for millions of Americans; with the avail-able tax credits, I currently pay less than $80 a month for my insurance. However, eligibility to buy insurance of the exchange is dependent on several factors, so make sure you find out if you qualify for ACA insurance before you quit your job to sell on Ebay.

If you are looking to Ebay to be your full-time income, you must examine the insurance costs involved as you will likely spend more on insurance than office supplies. And it is not just health insurance but also life insurance, injury insurance, sick time, vacation time, and retirement accounts. Again, you don't want to give up a good-paying job and benefits for an Ebay career unless you are 100% sure it will provide for you and your family!

If you are serious about making Ebay an actual business, it is definitely helpful to talk to someone with business experience. If you want to work from home selling on Ebay for a part-time or full-time income, two organizations can assist you: **SCORE** and the **Small Business Administration**.

SCORE stands for the Service Corp of Retired Executives. SCORE volunteers are former business owners who offer FREE, confidential counseling to anyone starting or expanding a business. They have 350 chapters in the United States, so you will likely be able to find an office near you.

Note that SCORE volunteers are retired and older; while they do have a lot of business experience, they may not know about Ebay or online retailing. However, they can definitely help you figure out any local or state laws regarding home-based businesses; and they will know some necessary information regarding taxes and permits. SCORE volunteers can also help you craft a business plan.

To learn more about SCORE and to find an office near you, visit **Score.org.**

The **Small Business Administration, or SBA**, offers confidential counseling and classes to anyone wanting to start a business, as well as services for those already running a company. SBA employees can provide you with information on what you need to operate a business in your area, including permits, licenses, and taxes. Most offices have a small library of business books you can borrow, as well as computer labs. Classes are incredibly low-cost. They also offer incubator spaces for businesses needing a start-up location. As with SCORE, SBA staff can assist you in writing up a business plan, which at the very least, is a guide to helping you along with your business, and at most is crucial if you want to get funding.

To learn more about the SBA and to find an office near you, visit **SBA.gov.**

What I Did: When I started my business, I signed up for a one-hour "Quick Start" class at the local Small Business Administration office. The cost was $15, and in the class, I learned that I only needed to register my business name with the city if I wanted to prevent anyone else from operating a business under that same name. In 2005, it cost me $17 to file my business name with my city. The class instructor also showed me how to get both a Sales Tax Permit and an Employer Identification Number, both of which I discussed earlier in this chapter. While I did get some necessary accounting information, they recommended consulting with an accountant, which I did (I will talk more about hiring an accounting coming up later in this book).

I followed up by phone and email with my SBA counselor a few times during my first couple of years in business. While I didn't end up needing a ton of help from the SBA, what they did provide me with was invaluable as it was the permits and taxes that had me so confused before I started.

As I mentioned before, the biggest mistake I see new Ebay sellers make is jumping into starting an Ebay business with both feet before educating themselves on not only Ebay itself but business in general. And while getting help from SCORE and the SBA is very helpful, since Ebay is a unique business that not many people in your area may be knowledgeable about, you will definitely want to seek out all the information you can on your own, including:

Books: When I started my business back in 2005, I read every book I could get my hands on. There are a ton of Ebay books out there; look for the highest-ranked ones on Amazon and buy or borrow from the library the newest editions. Ebay is continuously evolving, so you want to make sure you read the most up-to-date information out there. In addition to this book, I have written several other books about selling on Ebay (the link to my *Amazon Author Page* is at the end of this book).

Computers: To sell on Ebay, you need to have at least an intermediate working knowledge of computers. If your computer skills are rusty or if you have never used a computer in your life, don't fret. Most community colleges and even some libraries offer adult continuing education classes, including computer classes. Some even offer Ebay courses.

Ebay's Seller Help: Ebay itself is a fantastic resource for both new and experienced sellers. Check out the *Seller Help* link at the top of your *Seller Hub* page for articles, tutorials, and videos. When I started my Ebay business, I studied every single section on this site; and it helped me with everything from listing to shipping.

The Ebay Community: When I first started selling on Ebay, *The Ebay Community* (previously referred to as the "message boards") was a wealth of information for me. You will find the link to *Community* at the very bottom of all Ebay pages.

There are several sections of *The Ebay Community,* including:

- **Seller News:** Announcements and Seller Town Halls
- **Knowledge Base:** Buying & Selling Q&A, Commonly Asked Questions, and Community Mentor Corner
- **Discussions:** New To Ebay, Buying & Selling, Inside Ebay, Categories, and Seller Updates
- **Groups:** Ebay Categories, Business Insights, Regional Groups, Special Interest Groups, Payments, Ebay Upfront, Meetup Organizers
- **Ebay Podcast:** The Ebay for Business Podcast

Facebook: If you have a Facebook account, you will find many groups dedicated to selling on Ebay. The **Ebay for Business Facebook** page also posts on a daily basis; it's the best place to go to get up-to-the-minute announcements directly from the company. And you can join the private **Ebay for Business Podcast Group**, too.

Instagram: There is an active "reselling community" on Instagram that shares tips and tricks for selling on all of the online platforms, including Ebay. If you are new to Instagram, you can follow my account (which is linked on the last page of this book) and find other resellers through me. Whether you need specific questions answered or just want to find fellow resellers to connect with, you'll find a great community on Instagram!

YouTube Videos: Ebay has its own YouTube channel where they post videos of seminars from Ebay events. There are also a ton of reselling videos made by Ebay sellers, including myself. I have an entire YouTube channel, linked on the last page of this book, dedicated to reselling on Ebay. So many Ebay sellers are sharing their tips and tricks for making money on their own YouTube channels. Whether you are looking for tutorials, hauls, or thrift-with-me videos, you will find them all within the reselling community on YouTube!

CHAPTER SEVEN: EBAY ACCOUNTING MADE EASY

I get so many questions from Ebay sellers who, like me, are not very confident with their math skills. However, while it is important to keep adequate accounting records for your Ebay business, it really is not hard at all once you establish a basic system for your recordkeeping. In this chapter, I will lay out exactly how to make the Ebay accounting process as EASY for you as it is for me! Trust me, if I can keep my Ebay records using this system, so can you!

Should you hire an accountant?

Before we get to the actual accounting system, we need to cover some other important issues surrounding the finances of selling on Ebay, including hiring an accountant. Please note that these are my experiences; as with anything, be sure to do your own research on all aspects of your business, especially when it comes to accounting and taxes, as laws vary by state. When having doubts, it is always best to consult with a tax professional in your area.

When I started my business in 2005, I met with an accountant who set up the bookkeeping system I will be sharing with you in this chapter. The simple system he set up for me years ago still works for me today. It has stayed the same whether I was selling gift baskets locally, wholesale items on Ebay and Amazon, or secondhand items on Ebay, Etsy, and Poshmark. I knew my accountant well from my previous office job and have always trusted his advice and knowledge.

However, while I keep my own books throughout the year, I DO hire my accountant to file my taxes. Tackling my own tax returns is not something I personally feel comfortable with. Because I have an easy system for my bookkeeping, though, I simply keep track of everything throughout the year and then turn it all over to my accountant at tax time. Since I have kept good records for the year, he can quickly and easily file my taxes for me, which drastically cuts down on the bill he sends me for his tax filing services.

It is important to understand the difference between keeping your own accounting books and then hiring someone to file taxes versus hiring someone to do ALL of your accounting. I keep my own BOOKS, but my accountant files my TAXES. If my accountant kept my books for me AND filed my taxes on top of it, I would be paying him a hefty monthly fee. I do know some small business owners who meet with their accountants quarterly to manage their books. It really depends on the person and the business itself as to how often someone should meet with their accountant over the course of a year.

If you are comfortable filing your own taxes, you will still be able to use the accounting system I show you later in this book. However, if you want to hire someone to do them for you, you will save a lot of time and money by having your accounting system in place. That way, when tax time comes around, you can simply hand over your records to a tax professional, and they will be able to file them for you easily.

Again, the less time an accountant or tax preparer has to spend sorting out your records, the cheaper their bill will be. While it may be tempting just to save up all of your receipts and give them to someone a few days before April 15th, it is so much easier and cheaper to keep your own records and simply have someone file your returns for you.

There is no need for me to give my accountant a stack of receipts at tax time or for me to go over all of my credits and debits line by line as the system I use summarizes my gross sales and net expenses in one basic sheet of paper. I simply give him my accountant my gross sales totals and my expense totals using the easy accounting system I have in place, and he handles the rest. At this point, I could probably just follow my accountant's template and file my own returns; but I prefer the security of having a CPA prepare and file my taxes for me.

Whether or not to hire an accountant is a personal choice. I have to admit that I feel a bit safer hiring someone to file my taxes for me. The IRS loves to audit small businesses, and I feel that having an accountant handling my returns offers an extra layer of protection for me. I even sign a form that gives my accountant permission to talk to the IRS on my behalf if any questions arise.

Another bonus of hiring an accountant to file your returns is that they are specifically trained to get you the most deductions possible. Most Ebay businesses are run out of homes (mine is!), so there are many additional deductions available that aren't for people who run brick-and-mortar stores. I can deduct the space I use in my home for my business, including property taxes and utilities. I also get deductions for using my car for business. My accountant keeps all of this information in my file and just fills it in on my tax forms every year.

One final perk for me of having an accountant has been that he can set me up to pay my income taxes every quarter rather than all at once at the end of the year. Using the previous year's returns, he estimates what I may have to pay the following year. He then prepares tax forms for me to submit every three months. I simply cut a check and mail in the forms, both to my state as well as to the

Federal government. Sometimes I still end up owing a bit more money in taxes at the end of the year, but that just means that I MADE more money. And with the changing tax laws, occasionally I end up with a refund.

While it is nice to hope that you'll always get a tax refund every year, paying quarterly definitely protects you during the years when you may have underpaid and then owe money. Paying my income tax quarterly prevents me from getting hit with a potentially massive tax bill from the IRS at the end of the year. If, at the end of the year, it turns out I have overpaid on my quarterly tax returns, I will get a refund. And since I am not skilled in the IRS laws, I need my accountant to do this for me. When it comes to taxes, I would rather overpay than underpay as the IRS will eventually come to collect what they are owed!

If you do feel you need to hire an accountant or tax professional to prepare your taxes, be sure to ask around to your friends and family for their recommendations. There are many big accounting firms around that will charge you an arm and a leg to handle your returns. But many people run small offices or even work part-time from home who can do your taxes for a lot less.

Get recommendations from your friends and family, and then make a few calls. Ask what they charge for tax filing, and ask if they do free initial consultations. Also, be sure to ask if they have experience filing taxes for home-based e-commerce businesses, specifically Ebay, as they come with their own set of rules. If you use the accounting techniques that I will be sharing with you in this chapter, you will be able to tell potential CPA's that you keep your own books and are just looking for someone to submit your tax filings every year.

However, if the accountants you interview do offer a free or low-cost initial consultation, take advantage of it. If you have started keeping your own records, take them with you to the meeting to see if they can work based on what you have or if they want to make changes to your system. Having a good accountant on your side is never wrong when running a business; plus, you can write their fee off as a business expense!

If you feel confident filing your own taxes, you can skip hiring an accountant. However, note that it is good to educate yourself on your state's specific tax laws. A little research can save you a lot of grief at tax time. Fortunately, you can use two FREE resources: **SCORE** and the **Small Business Administration**, both of which I discussed earlier in this book. Most large cities have these services available; a quick Google search will bring up the offices closest to you.

Both SCORE and the SBA can advise you about the potential need for you to hire an accountant, and they can also help you determine whether you want to set up your Ebay business as a **sole-proprietorship** or **LLC.** The vast majority of Ebay business owners are sole proprietors, someone who owns an unincorporated business by themselves. An LLC is a business that has legally been set up as an organization. Different tax laws apply to each. There are more tax benefits with an LLC, but an LLC is much more complicated to set up and complex to maintain. If you are going to form an LLC, you will definitely have to hire a CPA to assist you.

Again, a SCORE volunteer, SBA employee, or an accountant can talk to you about whether a sole proprietor or LLC is best for you. Still, unless you plan to hire employees, you will likely be operating as a sole-proprietor. That means that you will be filing your business taxes under your given legal name.

As a sole-proprietor myself, my legal name is technically my business name as far as the IRS is concerned. However, my name is followed by D.B.A., which means "Doing Business As" on bank statements and permits. My Ebay store name, i.e., my business name, isn't really necessary, but as I've discussed previously, if you plan to purchase wholesale products to resell, having that D.B.A. shows that you are an actual business.

Note that a D.B.A. can also affect how you cash checks; most banks will only cash checks to accounts that match the checks' name, including the D.B.A. So, if you get checks made out to your D.B.A. name, a bank likely will not deposit them into an account that only has your name on it. This is something you will definitely want to check with your bank about. If they feel you should have an account under your D.B.A., it should be easy to set up and may even link to your personal account. Some banks may also require that you file a business license in your city with the D.B.A. name. If they do, don't panic as the process is simple and relatively inexpensive to complete at your local courthouse. Again, your bank will be able to best advise you on this.

If you plan just to flip finds from garage sales, though, I would not worry about having a D.B.A. You can certainly create a business name for the fun of it, but legally just your name will likely suffice. However, suppose you plan to grow your business beyond just a part-time gig. In that case, you will definitely want to consult a lawyer or your accountant to learn about the benefits of changing your business structure to an LLC. Even though my business has changed and grown over the years, neither my accountant nor I have felt it necessary to convert my business to an LLC.

Opening a Business Bank Account: The whole point of selling on Ebay is to MAKE MONEY! Therefore, it is a good idea to get a separate checking account dedicated solely to your business. Having a business account separate from your personal account makes keeping track of business income and expenses so much easier. As I discussed earlier, most banks will not cash checks that are made out to business names into your personal accounts. So, if you plan to be receiving any payments using your D.B.A. name, a business account might be necessary.

If you aren't already a credit union member, look for one in your area as they usually offer free account set up, free checking, and no ATM fees. You will want to get checks under your business account so that you can buy things such as office supplies directly from your business account. I write very few checks, but I sometimes use them at estate sales when purchasing inventory.

Having a dedicated credit card for your business is also a good idea. I have a credit card that I keep on file with Ebay as a back-up funding source and use it when I buy something on the site.

In the rare instance that I have to take a package to the Post Office for shipping (I do most of my shipping from home with the postage deducted directly from my Ebay balance), I use the credit card to pay for the postage. I buy shipping supplies locally from Staples and Sam's Club, and online from several different companies; all supplies are charged to my cards. I also use credit cards when buying inventory at thrift stores, and a few of the estate sale companies in my area also accept them.

Charging business supplies, services, and inventory onto one credit card makes it easy for me to track my expenses. I chose a business credit card that offered rewards, too, so that I get something back for using it. However, be careful to pay off your credit card balance every month, or you will soon be using all of your profits to pay for credit card fees. When I sold new gift items that I bought at wholesale, I had to order them using a credit card; and the fees definitely added up quickly.

Using one card is ideal as I can pull up the monthly statements online while doing my monthly bookkeeping. I can easily see what I spent, where I spent it, and what I spent it on, making it quick and easy to itemize my expenses.

My Easy Accounting System: Ah, here we are at the heart of this chapter: How to keep your Ebay accounting records. This system is really so straightforward; trust me, anyone can do it if I can do it. To say that math is not my strong suit is an understatement! But even I can do my Ebay books this way.

How much money can you make selling on Ebay? As much as you are willing to work for! Many people sell on Ebay just for some extra money. Some do it as a part-time job. And others have expanded it into their full-time income. However, bringing in any amount of money requires accounting. As much as you may want to avoid bookkeeping, trust me when I say that when tax time rolls around, you will be so glad you started and stuck with a system at the beginning of the year. You cannot hide from Uncle Sam; the IRS will eventually catch up with you. And this accounting system is just too easy not to do!

When I started my business, I paid my accountant $300 for an hour-long meeting in order for him to set up my bookkeeping system. And it is this EASY system that I am about to layout for you. Basically, it is just a check register, like the one you probably have in your checkbook. I keep track of my debits and credits and then hand off the totals to my accountant at the end of the year. You can use a computer spreadsheet, a paper bookkeeping book, or just a plain notebook. I use a lined paper notebook for my day-to-day records and then transfer the data onto a Word document on my computer. No fancy accounting programs for me!

Your business accounting breaks down into two categories: **DEBITS** and **CREDITS**

Debits are my expenses (withdraws) on the check register.

Credits are the funds I earn (deposits) on the check register.

While many people use a basic spreadsheet program such as Excel, I do things the old-fashioned way and hand-write my accounts. Yes, some of you may laugh; but writing everything down is much easier for me than typing it all in day after day. The only computer work I do is creating end-of-month reports and then combining all of that data into one year-end printout that I give to my accountant.

Using an account ledger (which can be found at any office supply store) or on a lined piece of paper, I write my categories across the top. The categories I use are:

Check # (I don't write very many checks, but I still include this column for the few I do)

Date (the date of the transaction)

Transaction (the transaction itself, such as "USPS" or "PayPal")

Debit (the amount of money I spent)

Credit (the amount of money I deposited into my account from PayPal or checks)

Balance (my total running balance after the most recent debit or credit)

And that is it! That is what I use to track my running day-to-day numbers. Yes, it looks just like a checkbook register and is very easy to keep.

At the end of the month, I break my numbers down further to itemize my expenses. Again, this can be done on a ledger or a piece of paper. Here is how I break down my numbers (I will use September as an example):

SEPTEMBER CREDITS:

Ebay Gross Sales: This number can easily be found by going to your **Seller Hub**, clicking on the **Performance** tab at the top of the page, and choosing **Sales** from the drop-down menu.

Other Gross Sales: If you sell on other platforms, such as Poshmark or Etsy, or if you sell locally via Facebook Marketplace or at an antique mall booth, you can break out those sales numbers here; since this is an Ebay focused book, we'll just stick to Ebay numbers for this example.

SEPTEMBER DEBITS/EXPENSES:

PayPal Fees for Ebay Sales: You can locate this number by logging into your PayPal account and selecting your monthly statement. Simply click on "Reports" at the top of the page; then click on "Statements" and select "Monthly." You can then generate a report of all your PayPal activity by month; the PayPal fees you paid are located under the "Fees" section.

Ebay Fees: You can find a break-down of your monthly Ebay fees under the **Performance** tab in **Seller Hub**; simply select **Summary** from the drop-down menu to access this data.

Simply pull up your Ebay seller account and your monthly invoice to find how much you owed in fees for each particular month. Note that this amount includes store subscriptions, listing fees, final value fees, and any other fees, such as those for *Promoted Listings*. You do not need to break down each of these fees for your records; you just need the grand total of all your fees for tax purposes.

Cost of Goods: How much you spent during the month on items to resell

Postage: The amount you spent on postage, whether paid by you or the customer, is also found in the **Summary** section under the **Performance** tab in your **Seller Hub.** Because your shipping costs were included in your gross sales number, it doesn't matter whether you or the buyer paid for shipping; you just include the **Shipping labels** amount for the month on this line.

Advertising: I include thank you cards in my packages, and occasionally I run Facebook and Instagram ads to promote my Ebay store.

Office/Shipping Supplies: The total amount I spend on everything from labels and printer ink to poly mailers and bubble wrap is added here.

Website/Internet Services: I add together my monthly internet fee as well as how much I pay for my phone.

Sales Tax: Since Ebay now collects sales tax from customers and remits it to each state themselves, I will be dropping this category starting next year.

Credit Card Fees: If you are using a business card for purchases, you will want to keep track of the fees you pay on the card.

Monthly Health Insurance Premiums: If you pay out of pocket for health insurance, include that amount here.

Prescription Drug Copays: Tally up your monthly prescription drug copays here.

Dr. Copays/Deductibles/Dentist: Keep track of any out-of-pocket expenses you pay for health care, including at the dentist.

Mileage: I use the app MileIQ to track my business miles easily.

I can also claim a portion of my home as office space; my accountant has that figure already stored in my files and inputs it into my returns every year.

Let's look at how I keep track of my transactions during the course of the month, using a purchase of office supplies as an example:

Imagine that I purchase copy paper for $10 at Staples on February the 11th. On the checkbook style ledger that I've created using a simple notebook, I write "2/11" under "Date" and "Staples" under "Transaction." Since I spent money, I write "$10" under the "Debit" column. I then subtract $10 from the current "Balance" to give me my new business account balance. See how this is done just as I would have if had I been using my household checkbook?

At the end of the month, I look through my "Debit" column. I add together all of the expenses related to "Office/Shipping Supplies" and enter that number onto my monthly expenses sheet. At the end of the year, I add up all of the amounts under "Office/Shipping Supplies" to get my total yearly expenses for that section. That final number, which goes onto my year-end sheet, is the only number I have to provide my accountant with. I do the same for the other expense categories, too, and I give all of the category totals to my accountant at the end of the year.

There are a couple of shortcuts I use to track my expenses. First, I keep all business charges on one credit card; that way, I only have to look through one monthly statement to see where I spent money on office supplies and at estate sales or thrift stores.

Second, Ebay provides many useful statistics that make tracking your sales, fees, and postage costs a breeze via *Seller Hub*. I used to manually add up every individual shipping charge, but now that number is provided to me in one line in the *Summary* section of my *Performance* page.

All of these numbers are essential to help you see how much money you are actually making by selling on Ebay. Figuring out your **NET** versus **GROSS** income is KEY to running any business.

GROSS income is the total amount of money, the "credits", you bring in BEFORE expenses are taken out.

NET income is the total amount of money you have let AFTER your expenses, the "debits," are taken out.

After you have accounted for all of your expenses, or "debits," you will have your NET income, which is the actual PROFIT you made. **GROSS minus EXPENSES equals NET PROFIT!**

At the end of the year, I total my monthly debits and credits and combine them into yearly totals. I give my accountant my GROSS sales number, which is the total of all of my credits. I then give him all of my EXPENSES, which are all of my debits. Subtracting my DEBITS from the CREDITS gives me my NET income for the year, and the NET income is what I pay taxes on. Since I have other sources of income (books, YouTube, affiliate marketing), I usually have several tax forms for my accountant to process. However, if your only business is Ebay, then you will either have the 1099 tax form Ebay provides you (if you sell over $20K) or the numbers you've kept yourself for your accountant to work on (or for you to process if you are planning on filing taxes yourself).

As I noted on my accounting sheet, I also have other deductions that I give to my accountant, such as self-employed health insurance and prescription drug costs. I can also claim the areas of my house that I use for my business, including the utilities and property taxes.

Another thing I claim is the mileage from driving to the Post Office and going to estate sales and thrift stores. An easy way to do this is to keep a small notebook in your vehicle and write down your miles anytime you drive around on business. Or, as I said, you can use an app such as MileIQ.

My accountant has set up for me an income tax payment system for me, where I pay quarterly. He prepares four forms for me every year so that every quarter I mail a form and a check into the IRS. That way, I keep up on my income tax throughout the year and don't get hit with a hefty bill when I filed my taxes. This is something he does as part of my yearly tax filing.

So, to recap: My accounting system is basically a check register where I log my debits and credits. I tally up the totals in each column at the end of the year and hand them off to my accountant, who then files my taxes. There is no big box of receipts to keep track of. I don't have to spend hours in my accountant's office going through my records. It takes me about 30 minutes a month and around an hour at the end of the year to add up all of my columns, and I then just give those numbers to my accountant. He factors in my deductions and files my tax returns for me.

EASY!!!

And to make it even easier for you, I also have yearly ledgers that I sell on Amazon. You can currently order my **2021 RESELLER PLANNER AND ACCOUNTING LEDGER,** which is an 8.5x11-inch book to help you keep track of your monthly and yearly sales and expenses. I also offer a smaller **2021 RESELLER MILEAGE LOG BOOK & PLANNER** that is small enough to fit inside of a bag or to leave in a car in order to track your on-the-go expenses and mileage. You can find both of these books in my Amazon Store at https://amzn.to/2HtrzBe.

Two questions I get asked a lot are, **"How much should I pay my-**

self?" and **"How much money should I reinvest in my business?"** After all of your expenses are accounted for, and you know your NET income, you will need to decide how much to keep for yourself and how much to put back into your business.

However, with Ebay, your sales, and therefore, your cash flow, can vary wildly, which makes answering these two questions nearly impossible. All I can really do in this instance is to share with you how I handle this division of paying myself versus reinvesting in my business.

After I fill out my accounting ledger at the end of the month, I see what my NET income for the month is. I pay all of my personal bills (not my business expenses, as those were deducted for me to get my net income) from that total, and I am then left with a new amount.

If it has been an excellent month of sales, I will have extra money to take out for myself while setting aside some for buying more items to resell. However, if sales have been really slow, I may find that there isn't much money left. So, I have to make a choice: put that money back in my business for supplies and inventory, or put it into my pocket for fun.

Let's say your NET income for January was $1000. Remember, NET means all of your business expenses, including fees and inventory, have already been deducted. Out of that $1000, you have $500 in personal bills that you need to pay, which leaves you with $500. After looking at prior months, you realize that you have spent around $300 a month to buy items to resell, so you decide to dedicate $300 to buy items in February, which leaves you with the remaining $200 for yourself.

Again, this is just an example. You always want to remember that you are selling on Ebay to MAKE money for YOURSELF! Keeping a ledger will help you track your cash flow and expenses to make an informed decision about how much money to take out for you and how much to leave in for your business. Don't get caught in the trap of reinvesting everything you make back into Ebay; be sure to PAY YOURSELF!

In business, you have to spend money to make money; selling on Ebay means you will be spending money on inventory and fees and supplies and taxes. In fact, during months where you are inventing a lot into your business, you may find that you barely break even...or even LOSE money. With that, here is some advice on how to save money when you are selling on Ebay.

1. Don't pay up for listing extras such as subtitles and second categories. Most of the "upgrades" Ebay offers aren't worth the money.
2. Repurpose shipping supplies when you can and ask friends, family, neighbors, and co-workers to give you their extra boxes and packing peanuts.
3. When you do purchase shipping supplies, buy them in bulk to save money.
4. Plan your car trips to cut down on excessive gas usage.
5. Pay with cash as much as possible. If you do use a credit card, use only ONE. And try to pay off the balance every month to avoid interest charges.
6. Don't invest in fancy backdrops and expensive camera equipment. I use a white poster board from the dollar store for photos and use my iPhone to take my pictures.
7. Don't go sourcing until what you already have is listed. Shopping for inventory is the best part about reselling, but if your items aren't listed, they can't sell. Your death pile is a money pile; don't bring any more items into your space until you list what you have.
8. Always look at the available shipping options for each order before purchasing postage to see if you can save a bit of money by choosing a different ser-

vice or carrier.

9. Utilize USPS FREE Carrier Pickup to pick up your Ebay packages to save a trip to the Post Office.

10. Don't invest in a fancy printer until you can pay for it in cash; I've run my business since 2005 without a DYMO, and you can, too.

BONUS: LIQUIDATION SOURCES

I f you sell on Ebay, you already know that thrift stores and garage sales are where most resellers find the items they sell. Buying items secondhand for pennies on the dollar will always net you the greatest return on investment.

But what if you could have brand new inventory delivered right to your door? That is where liquidation comes in! Liquidation companies deal in a variety of merchandise, including:

1. Customer Returns
2. Shelf-Pulls
3. Overstocks
4. Surplus
5. Damaged Items
6. Store Clearance

Most liquidation companies sell items by the case, pallet, or truckload; if you run your Ebay business out of your home, cases are the easiest to deal with as they ship in boxes that one person can lift. However, pallets are delivered by a freight company and require a large space, such as a garage, to process. And I am sure you can guess how much room a truckload of liquidation takes up!

If you are looking at purchasing liquidation to resell on Ebay, it is essential to research each of the companies you potentially want to order from to determine their policies and exactly what kinds of merchandise they sell. I only buy fully manifested lots that include a list of each item, including the brand, size, and original MSRP. I also only purchase liquidation that is in new condition. Note that "new" usually means that the original tags are still attached and that the item is unopened; these products may have been on the store shelves at one time and often come with clearance stickers on them, which you will want to remove before listing them for sale on Ebay.

Note that you will likely pay up a bit for liquidation items compared to what you pay at the thrift stores, but the cost makes up for not sourcing the products yourself at numerous different locations. And if you purchase new items, you won't have to do any washing or repair. I wash all secondhand clothing before I list it on Ebay, but I just get straight to listing when it comes to new-with-tags liquidation!

There are hundreds of liquidation companies out there; the following are the largest and best known. However, always do your own research before you order liquidation; just because a company is listed below does not mean it is a company you will be happy with. My best advice is to start by ordering a small case to test out a company so you can see if the items they ship to you actually match their descriptions. You can also note how the items were shipped and what their customer service is like.

Note that you must register with each of these companies to see their prices and policies; some require that you provide a state sales tax permit to purchase from them. Creating accounts with these companies will get you on their mailing lists for new inventory alerts and special offers, too. Most offer a discount on your first order when you register an account with them.

B&G TRADING - https://bandgtrading.com/: B&G Trading specializes in overstock, shelf-pull, and liquidation clothing from Macy's and Nordstrom's. They sell by both the case and the pallet.

BSTOCK.COM - https://bstock.com/: B-Stock connects you directly with liquidation sources at Amazon, Best Buy, Game Stop, GE, Lowe's, Macy's, Office Depot/Office Max, QVC, Walmart, Whirlpool, Sears, and JCPenney. Most of the sites they connect to are selling truckloads of merchandise via auction.

BULQ.COM - https://www.bulq.com/: Bulq.com sells liquidation from Target, Lowe's, and Bed Bath & Beyond, but the bulk of their items come from Target. They offer both cases and pallets with conditions of Brand New, Like New, Salvage, Scratch & Dent, and Uninspected Returns. Shipping on cases is $30; shipping on pallets is $200. They put up new lots every day, and they continuously mark them down until they sell. Bulq.com is an excellent source for cosmetics, toys, and consumer electronics.

CONTINENTAL WHOLESALE - https://continentalwholesale.com/: Located in Iowa, Continental Wholesale offers truckloads, half truckloads, and pallet lots of store liquidation from 16 different retailers.

DIRECT LIQUIDATION - https://www.directliquidation.com/: Direct Liquidation offers products from major retailers such as Walmart, Target, Lowe's, and Amazon in the form of auctions. They sell by the box, pallet, and truckload.

EBAY - https://www.ebay.com/: You are selling on Ebay, but did you know you can source on Ebay, too? There are hundreds of liquidation lots for sale on Ebay at any given time. Just search "liquidation" or "reseller box" to see what is currently for sale.

ETSY - https://www.etsy.com/: If you are looking to buy vintage items or craft supplies in bulk to resell, try Etsy. There are sellers advertising "wholesale" and "reseller lots" of all sorts.

FOX LIQUIDATION - https://www.foxliquidation.com/: Fox Liquidation advertises wholesale clothing from brands such as Ralph Lauren, DKNY, Lacoste, Tommy Hilfiger, and more. They call their cases "small wholesale lots" and their pallets "wholesale lots." Their website also features a clearance section.

GOODWILL BLUEBOX - https://goodwillbluebox.com/: In 2019, Goodwill launched their "Bluebox" website, which sells lots of clothing that didn't sell in stores and was headed to one of their outlet locations. As of this writing, Goodwill Bluebox is very new, and they sell out almost instantly whenever new stock launches. Hopefully, they'll grow the program as it is an affordable way source potential Ebay inventory. It's worth it to sign up for their email list and to follow them on Instagram for inventory updates.

HONCHO WHOLESALE - https://honchowholesale.com/: Honcho Wholesale offers liquidation by the case and pallet. They mainly focus on clothing from Macy's, Nordstrom, and Nordstrom Rack. All of their lots are fully manifested so that you know exactly what you are buying.

LIQUIDATION.COM - https://www.liquidation.com/: Liquidation.com offers a massive variety of goods to resell, including clothing, jewelry, electronics, computers, houseware, tools, and general merchandise. The twist is that the lots come from different sellers from across the country and are mostly available at auction. If you like hunting for deals, you'll love scrolling through Liquidation.com in search of lots to bid on.

LIQUIDATION GENERAL - https://www.liquidationgeneral.com/: Liquidation General specializes in high-end department store clothing. They also sell jewelry and specialty lots. Shipping on most of their lots appears to be free.

MERCHANDIZE LIQUIDATORS - https://www.merchandizeliquidators.com/: Merchandize Liquidators specializes in truckloads and pallets of cosmetics, clothing, housewares, and more. You can visit their headquarters in Miami Gardens, Florida, or buy from them online.

MIDTENN WHOLESALE - https://midtennwholesale.com/: Run by former Ebay sellers, MidTenn Wholesale sells a variety of merchandise from various sources in conditions ranging from brand new to salvage. Their lots are at a fixed price and range from cases to truckloads.

POSHMARK – https://poshmark.com/: Poshmark is an app (it's also accessible via computer) where people can buy and sell clothing. There is a whole community of Poshmark resellers, and some of them also offer wholesale/liquidation lots for sale. Try typing "liquidation," "wholesale," or "reseller lot" into the search bar to see what is available. Since Poshmark offers flat $6.95 Priority Mail shipping on packages weighing five pounds or less, expect only to find smaller lots for sale. But, again, it's an affordable way to test liquidation or buying in bulk.

QUICKLOTZ.COM - https://www.quicklotz.com/: Quicklotz offers cases, pallets, and truckloads at set prices that ship from three warehouses across the United States. They also sell Mystery Cases that ship for free within the Continental United States.

SOURCE LIQUIDATION - https://liquidation.source.com/: Source Liquidation is a liquidation marketplace that connects businesses with excess merchandise to resellers. All listings are auctions.

THREDUP – http://www.thredup.com/r/1W7XCF: While not a traditional liquidation company, ThredUp, which is on online consignment store, sells "Rescue" boxes. These mystery box lots contain items that weren't accepted for consignment or items that were listed but didn't sell. They offer clothing, handbags, shoes, and jewelry. You can also buy from them in bulk; email them at buybulk@thredup.com for more information.

VIATRADING - https://www.viatrading.com/: With lots starting at only $100, ViaTrading is an excellent option for testing out liquidation. They sell everything from brand new cosmetics to salvage appliances. If you are in the Los Angeles, California, area, you can even visit their warehouse and purchase pallets in person. They also have weekly on-site auctions.

WHOLESALE NINJAS - https://wholesaleninjas.com/: Wholesale Ninjas sells liquidation by the case, pallet, and truckload. They mainly sell cosmetics, toys, and clothing from Target and CVS. With box lots starting at around $100, Wholesale Ninjas offers an affordable way to test liquidation.

EBAY WHOLESALE DEALS: If you have an Ebay Store subscription, you can access the Ebay Wholesale Deals via the Manage My Store section under Subscriber discounts. Ebay Wholesale Deals is an exclusive marketplace where Ebay store subscribers can buy new or refurbished merchandise in wholesale quantities.

CONCLUSION

E bay is constantly changing and evolving. Their feedback system is continually being revamped, and new features, such as Global Shipping and Managed Payments, are always being added to the site. New buyer and seller requirements and standards are continually being rolled out, and every week seems to bring some new update to the site.

However, one thing about Ebay remains the same: Good selling practices are the best way to ensure your Ebay success!

By utilizing the tips and tricks in this book, you will be doing everything in your power to increase your Ebay sales. Of course, having a product that customers want is the first step; but taking care of your buyers is just as important. Detailed listings, great pictures, and stellar customer service are essential, as is utilizing all of the features Ebay has to offer.

Remember: Ebay is a TOOL you use in your business; it is not *your* business. Use the tips and tricks that I have provided to get the most out of the Ebay site, and you will see your sales and your bank account grow.

Selling on Ebay, while fun and profitable, is work. The harder you work, the more money you will make. Your business will continue to grow by following Ebay's rules and continually listing new items to their site.

Looking for more help with growing your Ebay business? Be sure to check out all my reselling books, all of which are available on Amazon on both Kindle and in paperback:

- BEGINNER'S GUIDE TO SELLING ON EBAY: https://amzn.to/34oFbX8
- EBAY SELLER SECRETS: https://amzn.to/3p6xKeT
- 101 ITEMS TO SELL ON EBAY: https://amzn.to/2Wqok1I
- 101 MORE ITEMS TO SELL ON EBAY: https://amzn.to/2LLIn8O
- Ebay Shipping Made Easy: https://amzn.to/2WzHv9f

Check out my reselling planners and journals:

- 2021 RESELLER PLANNER & ACCOUNTING LEDGER: https://amzn.to/3nzHMoE
- 2021 RESELLER MILEAGE LOG BOOK & PLANNER: https://amzn.to/2WDx70x
- MY RESELLER STORY GUIDED JOURNAL: https://amzn.to/3nw0jCm

Interested in starting a YouTube channel? Check out my book:

- HOW TO START A YOUTUBE CHANNEL FOR FUN & PROFIT: https://amzn.to/2KftrPN

ABOUT THE AUTHOR

Ann Eckhart is a writer, reseller, and online content creator based in Iowa. She has numerous books available about how to make money online and from home. Check out her Amazon Author Page at https://amzn.to/34nE9us for all her titles.

You can keep up with everything Ann does on her blog at www.AnnEckhart.com. You can also connect with her on the following social media networks:

FACEBOOK: https://www.facebook.com/anneckhart/

TWITTER: https://twitter.com/ann_eckhart

INSTAGRAM: https://www.instagram.com/ann_eckhart/

YOUTUBE RESELLING CHANNEL: https://tinyurl.com/yxvqtwc7

YOUTUBE VLOG CHANNEL: https://tinyurl.com/yxjqn6d2

Printed in Great Britain
by Amazon

23829761R00076